The Regulation of Cannabis in Europe

Changing attitudes towards cannabis across Europe are challenging old convictions of drug prohibition and making space for new approaches to the drug. This book delves into the evolving landscape of cannabis regulation across Europe and the world. Starting with Germany's push for full legalization, the work highlights the hurdles faced by policymakers, offering a detailed analysis of the international and European frameworks that restrict drug policy reform and discussing potential loopholes to avoid them. The case of Germany and its struggle with cannabis reform serves as a valuable blueprint with guidance for other states considering implementing more progressive approaches to drugs. The volume explores the complexities of cannabis regulation in a concise and approachable way, targeting not only legal professionals but also policymakers and readers with an interest in the societal dynamics of drug policy reforms and how these are shaped by the European Union and international law. The book will be of interest to a broad audience that includes legal scholars and practitioners; students of criminology, international law, and European law; and those with an interest in EU security and health policies.

Robin Hofmann is a criminal law scholar and criminologist currently working as an assistant professor at Maastricht University in the Netherlands.

The Regulation of Cannabis in Europe

Of Highs and Laws

Robin Hofmann

Routledge
Taylor & Francis Group
LONDON AND NEW YORK

First published 2025
by Routledge
4 Park Square, Milton Park, Abingdon, Oxon OX14 4RN

and by Routledge
605 Third Avenue, New York, NY 10158

Routledge is an imprint of the Taylor & Francis Group, an informa business

British Library Cataloguing-in-Publication Data
A catalogue record for this book is available from the British Library

Library of Congress Cataloging-in-Publication Data
Names: Hofmann, Robin, author.
Title: The regulation of cannabis in Europe : of highs and laws / Robin Hofmann is a criminal law scholar and criminologist currently working as an assistant professor at Maastricht University in the Netherlands.
Description: New York : Routledge, 2025. | Includes bibliographical references and index.
Identifiers: LCCN 2024061541 (print) | LCCN 2024061542 (ebook) | ISBN 9781032822037 (hardback) | ISBN 9781032822044 (paperback) | ISBN 9781003503439 (ebook)
Subjects: LCSH: Narcotic laws—Europe. | Drug control—Europe. | Cannabis—Law and legislation—Europe.
Classification: LCC KJE6191 .H64 2025 (print) | LCC KJE6191 (ebook) | DDC 345.4/0277—dc23/eng/20241230
LC record available at https://lccn.loc.gov/2024061541
LC ebook record available at https://lccn.loc.gov/2024061542

ISBN: 978-1-032-82203-7 (hbk)
ISBN: 978-1-032-82204-4 (pbk)
ISBN: 978-1-003-50343-9 (ebk)

DOI: 10.4324/9781003503439

Typeset in Times New Roman
by Apex CoVantage, LLC

Contents

Introduction

On 1 November 2022 something remarkable occurred on German public TV: The then German Health Minister Karl Lauterbach was invited as a guest to a popular German talk show hosted by Markus Lanz. Among the discussed topics were the government's plans to fully legalize cannabis, in which Lauterbach had played a leading role. The draft bill, however, was deemed as being not in compliance with European law and when questioned by the host, Lauterbach assured that if the new draft bill was not authorized by the European Commission, he would drop the entire bill, i.e., not go through with legalizing cannabis. Lanz replied sarcastically as to whether Lauterbach was hoping for the EU to disapprove, implying that the minister of health had gotten carried away with an impossible draft bill and was now looking for an easy way out of the project without suffering political damage. Lauterbach, however, wasn't having it and stood firm, even insisting that he was fully behind the law. At this moment, one can observe how the usually cool and rather polite Markus Lanz almost loses his composure for a brief moment and openly attacks his guest with the words, freely translated: 'You're not, Mr. Lauterbach. I've been listening to you for 30 minutes now and I can literally feel you arguing against your own inner convictions the whole time'.

What sticks out in this otherwise unremarkable TV interview is the fact that the hardened positions on the issue of cannabis legalization are condensed here as if in a burning glass: A health minister driven by somewhat naïve beliefs about the outcome and possibilities of legalizing cannabis is confronted by a talk show host who barely tries to hide his contempt and even claims to have full account of the true inner convictions of his guest. The clip was clicked over a million times on YouTube within a short time, showing the immense interest the topic of cannabis had sparked in the country. The health minister was visibly little amused about this accusation of acting against his own beliefs, but in the comments, he is widely praised for his courage to break new ground in German drug policies. Still, this interview must be seen as a turning point and marks the beginning of the end of German cannabis legalization. Only six months later, there was little left of Europe's most ambitious plan to regulate the soft drug. In April 2023, the legalization was significantly

DOI: 10.4324/9781003503439-1

scaled back to a partial decriminalization of cannabis and ratified by the German parliament about a year later.[1]

Still, this new German cannabis law is perhaps the most progressive in Europe, with a number of unconventional and problematic regulations. Lauterbach's law has managed to disappoint both supporters and opponents of legalization. While the former had hoped for comprehensive regulation with a free German cannabis market and dispensaries all over the country, it suffered a painful reality check. The latter were horrified by the far-reaching defusing of cannabis prohibition and ill-advised regulations. There is a saying that compromise is perfect when both sides are dissatisfied. Considering the law as the substrate of political compromises, one could conclude that the German cannabis law is the perfect law. Whether this is the case, how it all came about and what other countries can learn from Germany's experience with cannabis regulation are the subjects of this book.

It is no coincidence that the beginning of this book belongs to Karl Lauterbach, the German health minister, who, while not the initiator of German cannabis regulation, is associated with the failures and successes of the legislative process like no other. Interestingly enough, Lauterbach, who is a professor of medicine and a long-time member of the Social Democratic Party, was an outspoken opponent of cannabis legalization for most of his career. But then something changed, as he explained on the aforementioned talk show: During a conversation with a police detective, he was convinced that cannabis prohibition has widely failed and produces more harm than good. We don't know exactly what the detective told Lauterbach, but one can assume that criminal justice and criminological facts played a role. This is remarkable since medical issues surrounding cannabis have dominated the debate about the drug for a long time, and already, in 2017, Germany legalized medical cannabis.[2] It made me wonder what criminal justice and criminological arguments can be brought forward to end cannabis prohibition. Hence, this book will focus on criminal justice issues, crime policies, and criminological considerations in search of an answer to this question.

Germany's endeavor to tread new paths in drug policies gained traction in 2021 when the plan to legalize cannabis somehow found its way into the coalition agreement of the newly elected government. However, a plan of such societal aptitude doesn't come out of nowhere or develop in isolation. The legalization of cannabis for recreational purposes has been discussed in

1 The original wording can be found here: Bundesgesetzblatt Teil I 2024 Ausgegeben zu Bonn am 27 März 2024 Nr. 109, Gesetz zum kontrollierten Umgang mit Cannabis und zur Änderung weiterer Vorschriften (Cannabisgesetz – CanG).

2 BfArM. (2022). *Abschlussbericht der Begleiterhebung nach 31 Absatz 6 des Fünften Buches Sozialgesetzbuch zur Verschreibung und Anwendung von Cannabisarzneimitteln* (p. 4). https://www.bfarm.de/DE/Bundesopiumstelle/Medizinisches-Cannabis/Begleiterhebung/_node.html.

countries around the world for decades; still, in the vast majority of countries, cannabis remains prohibited. In an increasing number of states, however, cannabis is available for medical purposes. In a few countries, such as Canada, Uruguay, and some states in the USA, recreational cannabis is already freely available.[3]

Within the European Union, Malta and Luxembourg have opted in 2021 for what one could call a legalization light: There, it is allowed to grow a few cannabis plants at home for personal consumption. The sale in shops, however, remains prohibited. Portugal has implemented extremely progressive drug policies over the past two decades, while the Czech Republic seems to be on the verge of doing so. Then, of course, there is the Netherlands, with its world-famous coffee shops. Contrary to a widespread belief, cannabis is not legal there, but its sale is merely tolerated by law enforcement.[4] Denmark has toyed with some alternative approaches over prohibition and even tolerated the open sale of cannabis in Copenhagen's enclave Christiania. However, it almost seems that this experiment has come to an end, and a more similar approach to that of neighboring Sweden with its zero-tolerance policy towards all drugs has been implemented.[5] Indeed, some countries, particularly in the eastern part of the EU, have little enthusiasm for liberal drug policies.

Tracing Progression in Drug Policy Reform

One could achieve the impression that within Europe, there exists a patchwork of different approaches and policies when it comes to cannabis. On closer inspection, however, all these seemingly different policies are only marginally different and are all corralled under the same prohibitive umbrella provided by EU law, as this book will show. Germany has never been and still is no exception to this. The EU's largest country has not been famous for its liberal or progressive drug policies, with the exception of alcohol and, more specifically, beer, which can be consumed in public from the age of 16. Cannabis, like other drugs, was generally prohibited by law, with some exceptions for small amounts. Hence, many international and national observers were surprised when the new government, spearheaded by the Ministry of Health, pushed for a total legalization of cannabis in 2021. The initiative did not appear out of the blue but was preceded by years of careful legal

3 For an overview see Hofmann, R. (2022). Deutschlands cannabis dilemma. *Zeitschrift für Internationale Strafrechtswissenschaft*, 1(2).

4 Van de Bunt, H., & Muller, T. (2021). The bankruptcy of the Dutch cannabis policy: Time for a restart. In H. Nelen & D. Siegel (Eds.), *Contemporary organized crime* (Vol. 18, p. 14). Springer.

5 See e.g., Søgaard, T. F., Nygaard-Christensen, M., & Frank, V. A. (2021). Danish cannabis policy revisited: Multiple framings of cannabis use in policy discourse. *Nordic Studies on Alcohol and Drugs*, 38(4), 377. https://doi.org/10.1177/14550725211018602.

preparation by scientists, legal scholars, and politicians, especially from the German Green Party.[6] In this book, I trace this process, follow the crucial debates, address the arguments of the supporters and opponents of legalization, examine relevant court decisions, and show which legal and factual challenges the German legislature had to face. I will provide an overview of the relevant discussions in international and European law and also examine various regulation models in selected countries.

Many of the books dealing with legal issues related to cannabis prohibition, it seems to me, have a positive tone towards the drug. There is almost a kind of consensus among academics whether in the fields of health, law, or criminology: Cannabis legalization is progressive and the epitome of a modern drug policy. Of course, there are also opposing voices, but it seems these are a minority. Among the supporters are genuine experts and renowned scientists with differentiated and well-founded arguments. There are activists who see smoking pot as a civil right and prohibition as an arbitrary state action and a violation of human rights. For some years now, more and more lobbyists have joined the discussions, businesspeople who want to make money with cannabis. And, of course, there are those who simply like to consume their favorite drug, those who want to practice their hobby in peace and without fear of repression.

The societal debate on cannabis and the question if it should be legalized, on the other hand, is much more controversial, with many conservative politicians and considerable parts of the population opposing or being unsure if legalizing a drug is the right thing to do. Concerns regarding health risks and the protection of juveniles and children are frequently voiced against any plans of softening drug prohibition. These are valid concerns. But this book is not about cannabis as a health risk. In fact, there are a number of excellent medical studies by medical professionals.[7] Of course, the health risks of drug consumption cannot be left entirely out. Still, the analytical focus will be on legal issues and drug and crime policies. Drug policies are closely interwoven into international politics and relations, particularly into EU policies. The 'War on Drugs' declared by the US decades ago still shapes the global drug governance.[8] The international drug control regime plays a role, a bulwark of treaties standing strong against the smallest changes in the drug policies of the signatory states. And, of course, in this book, the jurisprudence of the Court of

6 See for example the first draft bill for a so-called cannabis control law here. Deutscher Bundestag, Drucksache 19/819 19. Wahlperiode, 20 February 2018.

7 See for example Hill, K. (2015). *Marijuana: The unbiased truth about the world's most popular weed*. Hazelden Publishing.

8 Hudak, J. (2020). *Marijuana – a short history* (2nd ed., p. 67 et.seqq.). Brookings Institution Press.

Justice of the European Union, as well as the European Union law in general, will play a role.

Drug policies, or, more particularly, cannabis policies as a sub-area of crime policies, are unique for many reasons: In few other areas, legislation is so dense and comprehensive while enforcement is so arbitrary and selective. In a few other areas, the ambitions of the law in the books and the societal reality are so contradictory. From a more philosophical point of view, one could formulate: How a society deals with drugs, with the problems and contradictions related to it, tells us a lot about us, how and why we punish, and how we define individual freedom.

Several Dilemmas

After establishing what this will be about, it remains to mention what this book is not and which readers might be disappointed: This book is not a plea for the legalization of cannabis or, even more so, all drugs. Those readers who are looking for confirmation of their worldview that smoking pot is cool and harmless and that the global prohibition policy is nothing but nonsense will be disappointed. But just as disappointed will be those who believe that smoking pot is the root of all evil and that a joint is only the first step towards a drug career that inevitably leads to addiction. Instead, the analytical benchmark of this book is evidence-based and scientific plausibility and not my personal or political worldview.

Still, in the spirit of full disclosure, I do believe that the better arguments speak in favor of legalizing cannabis for recreational consumption. I deliberately write 'believe' as I do not know for sure. And even after a thorough study of the scientific literature on the subject, I am far from certain that legalization is, in any case, the best solution to the problems we face with cannabis today. The title of this book points to the dilemma Europe is facing when it comes to cannabis. This is a dilemma that describes the situation where governments are eager to change their drug policies but are caught up in a spider web of prohibitive regulations and laws, reducing their room to maneuver to a minimum. As a legal scholar and criminologist, however, I find myself in another dilemma, one that is not related to the question of pro or con legalization but something more fundamental. On the one hand, like many scientists, I am risk-averse by nature, which means that I have a tendency to gather and analyze as much information as possible before making a decision or taking a position. The problem with complex issues like legalizing a drug is that the number of factors and possible outcomes is high, and the impact on society is unpredictable. Hence, the scientist in me says: In case of doubt and to be on the safe side, legalization should be put on hold until we have collected enough data to make an informed decision – knowing full well that we will probably never have enough data for a project of this magnitude.

But then there is the other side of the scientist. The side that has an affinity to experiments and asks: What if we legalized cannabis? What would happen? What would be the impact on society and people? How would we have to adapt our criminal law, and how could we even measure the effects of legalization? To be fully clear: Cannabis legalization in an EU member state like Germany would perhaps be the single greatest drug policy experiment of the last 50 years, maybe even of the whole century. The thought alone should make the heart of every scientist dealing with drug and crime policies beat faster – may it be out of enthusiasm or concerns of possible negative consequences. Either way, any experiment requires a strict definition of various parameters and framework conditions, as well as rigorous scientific monitoring and evaluation over the entire lifetime. Is Europe ready for this? This book is an attempt to find an answer.

1 The History of Cannabis – Medicine, Crop Plant, Safety Risk

Introduction

The history of cannabis is closely interwoven with the history of mankind. The origin of the plant goes back about 20 million years where the plan evolved from its two closest relatives, the hop (Humulus) and the hackberry (Celtis). Where exactly, how, and why this happened is the subject of controversial botanical debates. So is the question of when and for what reason humans first came into contact with the plant and how it spread across the world. Cannabis is an extremely adaptable plant. From the foothills of the Himalayas over the vast expanses of the Eurasian steppe to the warm subtropical zones, the cannabis plant feels at home. However, it prefers a warm, continental climate with plenty of rainfall in spring, an early and long summer, followed by a dry, cool autumn. Cannabis abhors a climate that is too cool or too humid.[1] It was a true multi-purpose plant for prehistoric man. Whether that purpose was medicinal, religious, or as a food or fiber plant, one use or another can be traced from early humans from Japan all over to Europe.[2]

There is some evidence suggesting that the cannabis plant split into fiber and intoxicant plants very early on. The early people twisted the fibers into ropes, nets, and textiles – all useful utensils, especially in the more northern parts of the world where alternative plants for textile production, like jute, are rare. Hence, in Europe, hemp has been cultivated for thousands of years. The plant spread from the Mediterranean regions to the rest of Europe during the Greek and Roman empires. Around 1150, the German Benedictine abbess and medical writer Hildegard von Bingen noted the healing powers of the hemp seed as being useful to reduce the bad juices of the body and strengthen the

1 Hill, K., & Ahmad, S. (2020). Chapter 2: The history of cannabis. In K. Hill & S. Ahmad (Eds.), *Medical Marijuana: A clinical Handbook* (p. 28). Wolters Kluwer. Much of the information contained in this chapter is taken from Hill and Ahmad's handbook, particularly The History of Cannabis.

2 Hill & Ahmad, 2020, 3.

DOI: 10.4324/9781003503439-2

good ones.[3] Although there are repeated references to hemp in medieval naturopathy, its importance was clearly in the production of goods. Above all, the emerging merchant shipping industry depended on the robust ropes made of hemp, but also inexpensive everyday textiles and even paper were made from it. However, there is little evidence that it was widely used as an intoxicant in pre-modern Europe. The reason for this might be that in most parts of Europe, mainly the fiber variant of hemp was available, which is very limited in its intoxicating properties.[4]

This changed when Europeans colonized the world around the 16th century. Through the interaction of Europeans with Asian and African cultures, hemp also became known in its drug variants as hashish, ganja, or bhang. In the early 19th century, Napoleon's troops brought hashish back to France from their Egyptian campaign. It enjoyed a certain popularity in artistic circles there – but it did not have a significant cultural influence.[5] Greater interest in the drug sparked among scientists in the Indian colonies. One of the better-known is maybe the Irish chemist William Brooke O'Shaughnessy (1809–1889). He worked for the East India Company in India in the 1830s and researched the medicinal effects of cannabis. His groundbreaking work triggered a wave of research, with over a hundred scientific publications on the subject in the coming decades.[6]

Cannabis use among the sepoys, Indian soldiers in the service of the British, aroused great concern among the colonial masters. According to press reports, the drug led the men on a direct path to crime and madness. A commission of inquiry hastily set up by the British could not confirm these findings and, moreover, advised against a ban on cannabis, as this would only fuel the smuggling of the drug. In 1893, another commission was set up to clear up the matter completely. This commission produced what was probably the most comprehensive study ever published on the effects of cannabis on humans: In seven volumes and on 3,500 pages, the statements of medical experts were collected, and the therapeutic as well as healing effects of cannabis were described. As a result, a prohibition of the drug was advised against, and moderate consumption was classified 'as harmless for body, mind and the moral kit that holds society together'. Excessive use, on the other hand, was described as dangerous for all three.[7]

3 Kastenbutt, B. (2021). Hanf: Geschichte und Gegenwart einer (Welt-)Kulturpflanze. In B. Kastenbutt, A. Lenaro, & A. Schmieder (Eds.), *Kulturdrogen – Drogenkulturen. Jahrbuch Suchtforschung* (Vol. 10, p. 79) LIT Verlag, Münster.

4 Hill & Ahmad, 2020, 43.

5 Hill & Ahmad, 2020, 44.

6 Hill & Ahmad, 2020, 46.

7 Hill & Ahmad, 2020, 38.

The Origins of Drug Prohibition and the International Drug Control Treaty System

At the end of the 19th century, hashish tinctures and pills were freely available in European pharmacies, while 'Indian cigarettes', a mixture of cannabis and tobacco, were offered as a remedy for asthma. Nevertheless, cannabis was still neither popular as a medicine nor a recreational drug in Europe. This was also due to the fact that at that time, synthetic drugs such as aspirin were increasingly coming onto the market, which were easier to dose and, moreover, ensured high profits for the pharmaceutical industry. But also as recreational drugs, the highly addictive morphine and later cocaine, which was developed as an antidote to morphine addiction, enjoyed great popularity. The comparatively harmless cannabis, on the other hand, was met with little interest.[8]

This changed at the beginning of the 20th century: Whereas the drug had hitherto been regarded with indifference or even with benevolence as a medicine, prohibitionism set in, slowly at first but gaining more and more speed. This dynamic was further accelerated by the fact that commercial hemp had also been losing importance for decades: The age of sailing ships with rigging made of hemp ropes had long since come to an end, and modern steamships used steel ropes.[9] Much has been written about the reasons for this rise of prohibition sweeping over all drugs, including the rather inconspicuous cannabis. Explanations range from religious prudishness to Protestant capitalism to open racism towards the often poor and non-white cannabis consumers. Probably all or even more reasons played a role leading to the outlawing of cannabis. At the turn of the century, something was changing in the way societies dealt with intoxicants.

In 1909, and following an opium crisis in China, which was fueled by the colonial powers, the International Opium Commission was founded in Shanghai and campaigned for an international ban on opium. At first, the colonial powers which were deeply involved in the opium trade were skeptical. They soon changed their minds: Opium increasingly spilled over from the Asian colonies to Europe and caused more and more problems there, too. In the port cities of Europe and North America, opium dens were widespread, where consumers could smoke the drug in a cozy atmosphere. This was also the case in the Hamburg Harbor in Germany, where Chinese sailors had opened such establishments. These 'dens of vice', which were also popular with Germans, operated behind the camouflage of green goods shops or laundries, and

8 Kastenbutt, 2021, 83.
9 Hill & Ahmad, 2020, 22.

although the police took action against them, opium dens are said to have existed in the city until the 1930s.[10]

In 1912, the colonial powers finally gave in, and it was agreed in The Hague at the first international opium conference that opium, morphine, and cocaine should be more strictly controlled. Cannabis, by the way, was not more than a footnote at this conference. The matter was adjourned, but the question of 'Indian hemp' was to be kept in mind and some years later in 1924–25 at the League of Nations Opium Conference in Geneva prohibition caught up on cannabis as well.[11]

In retrospect, this came as little surprise. The signs had already pointed to prohibition for the plant. Again, the British colonial power played a decisive role, but interestingly enough, not as an initiator of prohibition. The first country to ban cannabis was Egypt at the end of the 19th century. The British occupiers were skeptical about this move, fearing that it would only fuel smuggling. However, the Egyptian elites prevailed and became the pioneers of prohibition. South Africa followed suit in 1923, when police cracked down on people consuming the 'poor man's herb'.[12] At the opium conference of the League of Nations, cannabis was added to the list of controlled substances at the request of Egypt, Turkey, and South Africa. Against a popular belief, in the beginning, it was by no means the USA that was the driving force behind the ban on cannabis. Not only was the country not officially a member of the League of Nations at that time, the US representatives even left the conference early and consequently had little influence on the outcome.[13]

The conference resulted not in a full-fledged ban but rather in a compromise only obliging the contracting states to regulate cannabis for medical and scientific purposes, including the import and export of the drug. This was not yet an international prohibition regime. Germany, however, implemented the prohibition in the Opium Act in 1929. Commercial hemp was also affected by this, which may have been something like the final blow for the already struggling German hemp industry. During the Second World War, the industry was briefly revived: The durable and cheap hemp textiles were needed for German Wehrmacht soldiers. After the war, the ban was reinstated.[14]

10 Helmut, E. (1980). *Schwarze Chronik einer Weltstadt – Hamburger Kriminalgeschichte 1919 bis 1945* (p. 171 et.seqq.). Ernst-Kabel Verlag.

11 Collins, J. (2020). A brief history of cannabis and the drug conventions. *AJIL Unbound*, 114, 281. https://doi.org/10.1017/aju.2020.55.

12 Kastenbutt, 2021, 84.

13 Collins, 2020, 281.

14 Kastenbutt, 2021, 85.

The 'War on Drugs' and the Hippies

After World War II, the international prohibition regime as we know it today developed.[15] At the international level, psychotropic substances were increasingly regulated in a series of agreements, and these various treaties were transferred to the so-called Single Convention of 1961. For the first time, the term 'Indian hemp' was replaced by 'cannabis', and a distinction was also made between the resin and commercial hemp for industrial use.[16] In Chapter 3, we will take a closer look at the Single Convention, whose long shadow still falls on cannabis policy today.

From then on, the two major political guidelines of drug policy were: Criminalization and rehabilitating the users. Drug use became a criminal and a psychiatric-medical problem. The fact that these approaches can sometimes be in blatant contradiction to each other was certainly seen but also accepted. Nowhere is this more evident than in the famous American 'War on Drugs', declared by President Nixon in 1971. Of course, this was not a declaration of war in the formal sense but a symbolic one. But the rhetoric, strategies, organization, and financing of the 'War on Drugs' were strikingly similar to those of a real war.[17] It was a kind of general mobilization of society against the use of drugs and its consequences, such as crime and poverty. Nixon declared that America's 'public enemy No. 1' was drug abuse. Drugs quietly enter people's homes, destroy children, and erode the social fabric that holds neighborhoods and communities together. The fight against drugs required an offensive on all fronts of society and, of course, billions of dollars appropriated by Congress.[18] While this war was a unifying element between the political camps, it was also a political lever with which Nixon presented himself as a strong commander with zero tolerance for drugs and crime. The war, which was to be divided into a series of smaller and larger battles, was passed on from one president to the next. Although the respective 'Commanders in Chiefs' placed different emphases on the battlefield, the state of war itself remained untouched.

Cannabis, though not the top priority, has always been at the center of this war on drugs. While Jimmy Carter's administration was marked by cautious reforms, the pendulum swung back towards an intensified fight under Ronald Reagan. His administration pushed criminalization, stepped up the fight against smugglers, and increased penalties for the possession and consumption of cannabis and other drugs. At the same time, however, emphasis was also placed on prevention through broad-based educational programs

15 Duprez, D., & Groenemeyer, A. (2009). Drug use, drug problems and drug policies in Europe: History and current developments in international comparison. *Social Problems*, 20(1–2), 5–36, 15.

16 Collins, 2020, 282.

17 Hudak, J. (2020). *Marijuana: A short history* (p. 52). Brookings.

18 Hudak, 2020, 59 et.seqq.

and addiction treatment services. It was Reagan who expanded the war on drugs from a civil war across national borders into an international conflict. The DEA (Drug Enforcement Administration) intervened in the South American narco-states directly at the source of the drugs destined for the American market. Their toolbox ranged from spraying pesticides on drug farms to collaborating or breaking with some of the most feared dictators on the South American continent.[19]

Under Clinton in the 1990s, the war rhetoric became a little more moderate. Nevertheless, he continued to crack down on drug-related crime with the so-called three-strikes legislation which is most remembered. This was a provision that automatically provided for life imprisonment for repeat offenders on their third conviction, especially for violent crimes or drug trafficking. Clinton also massively increased the budget for the penal system and the police and intensified the fight against cannabis. By the end of his term, arrests for cannabis possession had doubled to almost three-quarters of a million annually. Ultimately, it was Clinton who also paved the way for the legalization of medical cannabis.[20]

The 'War on Drugs' is certainly a specifically US-American phenomenon. However, due to the internationalization under Reagan, the conflict left enormous traces, especially in South America, but also left its mark on the international drug treaty regime. Countless books, films, and entire series are set against the backdrop of the War on Drugs, and its cultural significance cannot be overestimated. Nixon's declaration of war also boosted the hippie movement. The public use of cannabis, but also LSD, was suddenly seen as a political statement and part of a counterculture. Until then, consumption had mainly taken place in secret. However, cannabis use not only took place in public but also gave rise to new black-market structures and types of dealers.

Cannabis Today

According to the United Nations Office on Drugs and Crime (UNODC) figures, in 2020, more than 4% of the world's population aged 15–64 (or 209 million people) reported having used cannabis in the past year.[21] Compared to 2010, this is an increase of 23% (there were 170 million people then, although the world's population was also slightly smaller). The prevalence of cannabis use varies quite a bit by world region, being highest in North America, Australia, New Zealand, and West Africa. Europe is more in the middle, and even within the European countries, there are some differences. According to a recent survey in Germany, more than 46.4% of young German

19 Hudak, 2020, 67 et.seqq.

20 Hudak, 2020, 77.

21 UNODC. (2022). *World drug report 2022, drug market trends cannabis opiods* (p. 14). UNODC.

adults (between 18 and 25 years) have used cannabis at least once in their lives. Among young people between 12 and 17 years of age, 10.4% have used cannabis at least once.[22]

Surveys on consumption are of interest from the point of view of health policy, but these data are not very meaningful, for example, with regard to questions of criminal policy: Which drugs are in circulation? How big is the black market, and which police measures are effective? One indicator that can be used to map these developments in the drug market is, therefore, data on the quantity of drugs confiscated. For example, data from the European Union Drug Agency (EUDA, former EMCDDA). This EU agency has recorded a 278% increase in herbal cannabis seizures in Europe since 2010.[23] However, these numbers have to be taken with a pinch of salt as confiscations only very inaccurately depict how drug markets actually develop. For example, the number of confiscated drugs can rise sharply when police and customs take stronger action against trafficking without the amount smuggled or produced actually increasing. The more you control, the more you will find. On the other hand, the number of drugs in a black market can snowball without the police noticing and without the confiscated amount changing. The bottom line is that we only have fairly rough ideas about drug markets. This is the nature of black markets: They are hidden and hard to control. More about this in the following chapter.

Conclusion

'Just say no!' This probably most famous slogan of the 'War on Drugs' was reportedly coined by First Lady Nancy Reagan, who, during the '80s, had made a name for herself by campaigning against drugs. During a school visit, a student was asked how to behave when friends used drugs: 'Just say no' was her answer.[24] This sentence demonstrates a simplified understanding of one of the most complex societal problems and a remarkable optimism about controlling the problems. This optimism has faded.

Today, there is much more to say about the history of cannabis, its impact on societies, and the implications of the war on drugs, especially for societal minorities. The latter issue, respectively the interdependencies of cannabis and law enforcement, has gained increasing attention in the scientific literature over the past years. Although scientific studies have contributed to a better understanding of these highly problematic social dynamics, the issue has received much less attention in the European context, especially in the

22 Orth, B. & Merkel, C. (2020). *Die Drogenaffinität Jugendlicher in der Bundesrepublik Deutschland 2019. Rauchen, Alkoholkonsum und Konsum illegaler Drogen: Aktuelle Verbreitung und Trends. BZgA-Forschungsbericht* (p. 8). Bundeszentrale für gesundheitliche Aufklärung.

23 EMCDDA. (2022). *European drug report 2022: Trends and developments* (p. 21). EMCDDA.

24 Hudak, 2020, 67.

German scientific discourse.[25] While there is still a lot of catching up to do in this respect, the topic goes beyond the scope of this study.

Some other pressing issues, however, will be addressed in later chapters of this book. The war on drugs, with all its social implications, is certainly not a purely American phenomenon. Many of this war's dynamics can also be seen in Europe, albeit in a somewhat weaker form. For the legal analysis that follows, the war on drugs provides something of a canvas on which the images of contemporary drug policies in Europe have been painted. The context of this war is particularly important for understanding the international prohibitive system, which we will delve into in Chapter 3.

25 For a good overview from a criminological perspective and further sources, see Wheeldon, J., & Heidt, J. (2023). Cannabis and criminology: A history of race, addiction, and inconvenient research. *Journal of Criminal Justice*, 85.

2 The German Cannabis Controversy

Introduction

There is probably no other drug that has been and still is discussed as much and as passionately as cannabis. Since the end of the 1960s and the hippie movement, smoking pot has been an expression of a youthful counterculture, a peaceful rebellion against social conventions. With cannabis becoming more and more mainstream, demands for its legalization were voiced with increasing vehemence. Interestingly enough, this is not just from the consumer or the stoner scene, but from scientists, politicians, human rights activists, economists, lobbyists, and political activists. Although these legalization advocates are well networked, have good arguments, and have a powerful lobby with immense influence, remarkably, over decades, very little moved towards legalization. This has changed in recent years.

In Germany, the first actual changes in drug policies were observed around the beginning of the 2000s. This chapter delves deeper into the debates that ultimately led to an entirely new approach towards cannabis. Questions that will be addressed are: What sparked that change in drug policies? Which role did global developments play? What role did the fact play that cannabis started a career as a medical product? How did this health debate influence the question of legalizing cannabis for recreational use? How did this impact consumption patterns? What effects are expected from legalization? And why, despite all these changes, is the topic of cannabis still so controversially discussed?

While the focus will be on the German debate, global developments will be included in the analysis. To understand the legal aspects and obstacles related to cannabis regulation or drug prohibition in general – which will be addressed in the subsequent chapters – it is paramount to keep the underlying societal and political debate in mind. Very roughly spoken, the debate is split into two closely interwoven lines of reasoning, which, when mixed up, are responsible for many of the misunderstandings that exist between supporters and opponents of cannabis. One line of reasoning revolves primarily around health aspects, i.e., around questions of how harmful consumption may be and if cannabis even has medical properties. Proponents of that debate are mostly

DOI: 10.4324/9781003503439-3

health professionals; their focus is on drugs as a health-related issue. Separate from this is a debate on criminal policy and cannabis as a problem to societal security. In essence, it is about why we criminalize certain behaviors like drug possession, how effective criminal justice systems can enforce such a ban, and if and how deterring effects can be measured on consumers and potential consumers. The focus of the following analysis will be on the latter. However, since the lines of argumentation are deeply intertwined, questions surrounding the impact of cannabis on health should and cannot be ignored entirely.

The Health Debate on Cannabis

Most people only come into contact with drugs in crime shows on TV. There, it's about dealers, police officers, and addicts who slip into crime to finance their addiction. Or it is about drug gangs and big cartels that amass fabulous wealth through bloody violence and corruption before inevitably crumbling under the force of the law. Drug-related crimes are an interesting and important issue, but it seems that the public debate about cannabis mostly revolves around health-related issues. The reason for this is that, over time, our view on drugs and addiction has changed. Not too long ago, drug addicts were merely viewed as criminals and as risks to societal security, which were best handled by the criminal justice system. This view has largely changed to the point where the term 'addiction' alone is considered stigmatizing, and the terms 'dependence' or 'substance use disorder' are favored.[1] Modern health approaches to drugs consider drugs first and foremost as health risks and addiction as a disease treatable by the health system. While this is a rather simplified view on a very complex issue, a growing number of authors have a rather critical view of this disease model health approach.[2]

While this is an ongoing academic and medical discussion that should not concern us at this point, the question remains: How harmful is the consumption of cannabis to human health? This, of course, is a very different question from the question we addressed in the previous chapter on the history of cannabis, if and how cannabis can be used as a medicine. In fact, there is a lot of controversy around this question of impact on health, and the question is anything but easy to answer. There is no scientific consensus on the risks related to cannabis use. Hence, Caulkins et al. notice that 'both sides of the legalization debate can and do refer to published studies that support their arguments and claim that the other side is "ignoring the science"'.[3] Therefore,

1 Caulkins, J. P., Kilmer, B., & Kleiman, M. A. R. (2016). *Marijuana legalization: What everyone needs to know* (2nd ed., p. 25). Oxford University Press.

2 Lewis, M. (2017). Addiction and the brain: Development, not disease. *Neuroethics*, 10, 7–18. https://doi-org.mu.idm.oclc.org/10.1007/s12152-016-9293-4.

3 See Caulkins et al., 2016, 22.

their advice is to acknowledge uncertainties and remain open-minded while avoiding surrounding oneself only with people who are like-minded in these matters – advice the author of this book could not agree more with.

The lowest common denominator seems to be that cannabis can be somewhat harmful to health. It has this in common with probably all other drugs. However, there is disagreement about how these health risks should be evaluated, i.e., how dangerous cannabis actually is for humans and how addictive it can be. While some consider the so-called toxicity to be low, others warn of the considerable physical and psychological side effects that can result not only from regular but even one-time use. Particularly, the specific effects on young people and their underdeveloped brains play a role in the discussion.

The fact that opinions differ so widely may be surprising, but it is not unusual for a scientific debate. This is further complicated by the fact that, due to the illegality of the drug, there are relatively few studies that deal in depth with long-term use and dependence on cannabis.[4] In addition, cannabis is a rather dynamic drug. The weed that is available on the black market today often has little to do with the harmless hippie drug of the '70s. More and more so-called synthetic cannabinoids have seeped into the market in recent years. These can be significantly more potent than natural hemp herbs, and thus can be potentially much more harmful to health. In addition, the phenomenon of black-market dealers stretching cannabis with other sometimes highly poisonous substances in order to maximize profits has increasingly become a problem.

The Health Effects of Cannabis Use

The Federal Agency for Civic Education (Bundeszentrale für Politische Bildung), a federal public authority in Germany providing citizenship education and information on political issues, writes about the known side effects of regular cannabis consumption:

> *The 'amotivational syndrome' is often described, an increasing lack of interest and drive; deterioration of memory and attention are documented. In addition, cannabis smokers develop schizophrenia much more frequently, often directly after acute intoxication. In addition, there is damage to the mouth, throat and bronchial system, because the combustion of marijuana leaves produces even more toxic products than tobacco.*[5]

4 Hoch, E., & Preuss, U. W. (2021). Cannabis, Cannabinoide und Cannabiskonsumstörungen. *Suchttherapie*, 22(4), 203–216.

5 Köhler, T. (2021). *Der Preis des Highs – Erwünschte und unerwünschte Wirkungen psychotroper Substanzen. Aus Politik und Zeitgeschichte*. Bundeszentrale für Politische Bildung.

The scientific literature reports increased risks for psychoses, depression, bipolar disorders as well as anxiety disorders due to cannabis consumption.[6] In addition, withdrawal symptoms can occur, especially with strong synthetic cannabinoids, which can lead to severe nausea, stomach pain, and even seizures. That these side effects may not just be rare and isolated cases is shown by data from the EUDA, as well as the current drug report of the UNODC. The EMCDDA's annual published European Drug Report estimates the number of people entering specialized drug treatment for cannabis-related problems in Europe in 2020 at 80,000. More than half of them (43,000) did so for the first time in that year.[7] The United Nations World Drug Report of 2022 even explicitly mentions Germany as a case study to point out the dangers of health damage in connection with increasing cannabis use. According to the UN data, between 2000 and 2018, the number of treatments for mental and behavioral disorders due to cannabis use increased more than eightfold in Germany, while the number of addiction and withdrawal treatments has more than quadrupled in the same period.[8]

In Germany, according to official addiction aid statistics 2021, about 22,500 men and 4700 women were treated for cannabinoid use on an outpatient basis in addiction aid facilities.[9] For men, this corresponds to about 22% of all outpatient treatment cases for addiction problems. Among women, this share is 13%. Unsurprisingly, the front-runners among these outpatient treatment cases are cases due to alcohol abuse. Among men, the number of cases is more than twice as high (approx. 46,500), and among women, even four times as high (approx. 20,200). However, it is remarkable that clients with cannabis-related disorders in addiction help centers have the youngest average age of 25 years. By comparison, alcohol clients are on average more than 20 years older (with 46 years on average).

These empirical data do not exactly put cannabis in a positive light. However, one should interpret these numbers with caution. For example, the strong increase in people seeking help in addiction facilities mentioned by the UN report is not only due to the increased number of users. The expansion of support services for addicts is likely to have had an effect on this as well, not to mention the increasing normalization of cannabis and, hence, the increased openness of consumers to make use of addiction support services. Today, users are much more willing to seek professional help without the fear of stigmatization, which one should consider a rather positive development.

6 Hoch & Preuss, 2021.

7 EMCDDA. (2020). *Drug report 2020* (p. 26). EMCDDA.

8 UNODC. (2022). *World drug report 2022, drug market trends cannabis opiods* (p. 24). UNODC.

9 IFT Institut für Therapieforschung. (2022). *Männer und Frauen in Einrichtungen der ambulanten und stationären Suchthilfe. Kurzbericht Nr.1/2022 – Deutsche Suchthilfestatistik 2021.* https://www.suchthilfestatistik.de/publikationen/kurzberichte.html.

But this does not mean that the developments reflected in the statistics are not worrying at all. It is well known that cannabis products available on the black market contain an increasing amount of THC, while the popularity of synthetic cannabinoids has increased enormously. The health risks of smoking pot have thus increased, leading to more consumers requiring professional support.

In sum, many things related to cannabis use remain controversial among health experts. The bottom line is cannabis, like any drug, is by no means harmless. The active substance THC has the potential to cause psychological dependence. The side effects, especially of regular and long-lasting use and the use of very potent cannabis products, can lead to considerable health impairments. Cannabis should, therefore, not be trivialized. But neither is it appropriate to demonize the soft drug. The mere existence of potential health risks does not mean that consumption should be unconditionally avoided, and the drug generally prohibited. Alcohol is a widespread drug whose pervasive negative effects on human health have been sufficiently and scientifically proven. The fact that it is still abused by an alarming number of people does not mean that prohibition is the only possible answer to the problem.

Ex Course: Medical Cannabis and the Break in the System

While the health-related risks of cannabis use have been known for a long time, developments in the field of medical cannabis have been more recent. While numerous countries allow the use of cannabis for medical purposes, in Germany, this has been the case since 2017. Despite this the status of cannabis as a medicine remains somewhat shaky, at least in Germany. The German Federal Institute for Drugs and Medical Devices (Bundesinstitut für Arzneimittel und Medizinprodukte, short BfArM), a federal agency responsible for licensing registration of medicinal products and monitoring of legal narcotics, considers the approval of cannabis as a medicine a 'breach of the system'.[10] In other words: It is unprecedented that patients are treated with cannabis for various diseases while its efficacy and safety have not been proven in clinical trials. Almost five years after factually approving medical cannabis, the Institute concedes that still, no findings from clinical studies exist that may justify

10 BfArM. (2022). *Abschlussbericht der Begleiterhebung nach 31 Absatz 6 des Fünften Buches Sozialgesetzbuch zur Verschreibung und Anwendung von Cannabisarzneimitteln* (p. 45). https://www.bfarm.de/DE/Bundesopiumstelle/Medizinisches-Cannabis/Begleiterhebung/_node.html.

the approval. Instead, one is pleased with the fact that clinical trials in 2022 have also begun in Germany. And further:

> *The goal must be to prove the efficacy and safety of cannabis medicinal products in clinical trials and to strive for the approval of finished medicinal products in order to remedy the breach of the system.*[11]

Recreational cannabis and the debate on full legalization have gained considerable momentum.

The first thing that is important to acknowledge when considering cannabis as a medicine is that the plant consists of different substances. In the chapter on the historical use of cannabis, it was already mentioned that a medicinal effect is mainly known from the cannabinoid CBD which is used for a wide range of complaints. While for some of these complaints, the efficacy has been proven in clinical trials, it is worth mentioning that the intoxicating effect of CBD is rather low. The opposite is true for THC, the famous cannabinoid which makes one high. THC as well is used against a whole range of complaints, including the treatment of chronic pain, spasms, and multiple sclerosis, as well as nausea, vomiting, and loss of appetite. In addition, THC may be used to treat insomnia, ADHD, and even intestinal diseases. THC-containing drugs are available in various forms, such as nasal sprays or capsules whose intoxicating effects are considered to be low. Most commonly, THC is inhaled by burning the cannabis flower in the classic joint or – more recently – by using a vaporizer to burn cannabis oil.[12] However, it is the cannabis flower containing THC which the German Institute is referring to as lacking scientific backing for its medical efficacy. Nevertheless, it was exactly this form of cannabis that sparked the medical debate in Germany as early as 2005.

Medical Cannabis Paving the Way for Full Legalization

To understand why the German Institute was willing to approve cannabis as a medicine despite the absence of clinical studies proving its efficacy, a closer look at the jurisprudence is useful. The Institute justifies this step in 2022 in order to prevent patients for whom no other medicines are available from self-medicating with black-market cannabis. This is based on the foundation laid by the German Federal Administrative Court already in 2005 for the availability of medical cannabis to patients. The court had ruled that a multiple sclerosis patient was entitled to medical cannabis even though the Federal Institute for Medicinal Products had initially rejected authorizing an

11 BfArM, 2022, 46.
12 For a full overview see BfArM, 2022, 12 et.seqq.

exemption. The latter was necessary as cannabis had not been approved as a medicine yet. The Institute had argued that such an authorization had to be in the public interest, while this was not the case for an individual patient. The Federal Administrative Court took a different view and argued that the public interest was completely irrelevant when it came to the health of an individual person.[13] From then on, the Institute was required to issue exemptions for medical cannabis at least as long there were no alternative therapies.

Nine years later, in 2014, the Administrative Court of Cologne further expanded the rights to medical cannabis and ruled in a landmark decision that a seriously ill man was not only allowed medical cannabis but to grow and consume his own cannabis. The court's argument was based on fundamental rights enshrined in the German constitution (the Grundgesetz or Basic Law). The state has a duty to protect the fundamental right to life and physical integrity under Article 2(2) and to uphold human dignity in the sense of Article 1 of the Basic Law.[14] Interestingly enough, the patient had very well the possibility of obtaining medical cannabis by obtaining an exemption from the Federal Institute for Medicinal Products. Hence, he could have bought it at a pharmacy for 15 € per gram – costs that were not covered by the health insurance. The monthly costs for the severely ill man amounted to 1500 €, which he claimed that he could not afford. So, he preferred to grow cannabis for self-medication in his own bathroom, and the court of Cologne considered this to be within his fundamental rights.[15]

The Federal Institute was thus forced into action if it wanted to avoid further defeat in courts. But issuing more exemptions or acting more generously to patients was no option since this would not have solved the problem of the considerable costs of cannabis that patients would have had to bear themselves. And advising seriously ill patients to just grow their cannabis seemed impracticable and rather inhumane as well. The simple solution was to approve cannabis as a medicine. Since then, doctors can prescribe a maximum of 100 grams of cannabis flowers for a period of 30 days. The health insurance company may only refuse to cover the costs in justified exceptional cases. According to Technikerkrankenkasse, one of the biggest German health insurance companies, the costs for cannabis therapies can be surprisingly high with 22 € per gram of cannabis flower, amounting to therapy costs between 300 and 2,200 euros per month. Therapies with opiates, on the other hand, are considered much cheaper.[16]

13 BVerwG 3 C 17.04, 19 May 2005.

14 Administrative Court Cologne Judgement, 8 July 2014 – 7 K 4020/12.

15 Administrative Court Cologne Judgement, 2014.

16 Information available on the Technikerkrankenkasse. https://www.tk.de/techniker/gesundheit-und-medizin/behandlungen-und-medizin/cannabis-verordnung-was-beachten-2032620?tkcm=aaus.

In conclusion, the court jurisprudence paved the way for medical cannabis, leaving the Federal Institute for Medicinal Products few alternatives in order to prevent seriously ill patients from being forced onto the black market. This stance of German courts to consider the therapeutic use and self-cultivation of cannabis as a fundamental right did not only provide the debate around recreational cannabis with new momentum. It was also unorthodox from a legal historical point of view as the German Constitutional Court already in 1994 had issued a final decision on the German approach to cannabis.

Kein Recht auf Rausch – No Right To Be Intoxicated

The debate about cannabis in Germany reached its first peak and, at the same time, its preliminary endpoint in 1994. Back then, several German courts had expressed doubts about the compatibility of the cannabis prohibition enshrined in the German drug law (BtMG) with the German constitution and appealed to the federal constitutional court to clarify this issue. In essence, the questions were the following: Is the difference we make between alcohol, nicotine, and cannabis an unequal treatment prohibited under Article 3 of the German constitution? Are furthermore those who want to get intoxicated and forced to use alcohol (since cannabis is prohibited) impaired in their bodily integrity protected under Article 2 of the constitution? In short, is the right to be intoxicated protected by the German constitution?

Not surprisingly, the court was not convinced and decided that cannabis prohibition was in line with the German constitution. According to the judges (with two descending opinions), a right to be intoxicated simply does not exist. The court explains:

> *Art. 2 para. 1 GG protects every form of human activity regardless of the importance of the activity for the development of the personality. However, only a core area of private life is absolutely protected and thus removed from the influence of public authority. This does not include the use of drugs, especially intoxication, due to its diverse social effects and interactions. There is therefore no 'right to intoxication'.*[17]

In addition, the court grants the legislature considerable discretion when it comes to drafting laws to protect public health. In the somewhat cumbersome words of the court, it sounds like this:

> *The aim is to shape social coexistence in a way that keeps it free from the socially harmful effects of dealing with drugs, such as those caused by the*

17 BVerfG 90, 145, 9 March 1994, lit 119.

> *so-called soft drug cannabis: Through it, young people in particular are introduced to intoxicants; their habituation to intoxicating substances is promoted. The consolidation of the personality of young people and adolescents can be hindered.*[18]

The decision was criticized, especially for its recurrence of public health (*Volksgesundheit*), a vague and diffuse legal concept with roots back to the era of national socialism.[19] Either way, the court decision of the highest German court put an end to the discussion for the time being.

Approximately 20 years later, the discussion gained new momentum, and it took another half a decade and a change of government in 2021 to turn the entire German prohibitive regime on its head. The Conservative government was replaced by a grand coalition of Social Democrats, Liberals, and Greens whose coalition agreement contained the single sentence:

> *We are introducing the controlled supply of cannabis to adults for recreational purposes in licensed shops.*[20]

One doesn't have to be a drug expert to understand that this sentence means no less than a full legalization of cannabis, including the production, supply, and selling of cannabis to German consumers. At the same time, numerous court cases were pending at the German Constitutional Court once again questioning the constitutionality of the cannabis prohibition. And once again, and in a remarkably concise decision, the German Constitutional Court brushed off these new attempts to declare cannabis prohibition unconstitutional by stating that no legally relevant changes to the factual and legal situation have occurred since its decision in 1994.[21]

Hence, the political ambitions of the governing coalition and the legal situation interpreted by the highest German court could not have been further apart. What were the reasons for this political stalemate? To answer this question, it is worth looking at the political debate about cannabis legalization in Germany.

18 BVerfG 90, 1994, lit 126.

19 Beulke, W., & Schröder, S. (1991). Abgabe von Rauschgift und bewußte Selbstgefährdung. *NStZ*, 393–394. See for the discussion Adam, J. (2020). *Die Rechtsgüter des BtMG und das Recht auf Selbstgefährdung: Konfliktlinien dargestellt am Beispiel des gemeinsamen Drogenkonsums unter besonderer Berücksichtigung von § 30 Abs. 1 Nr. 3 BtMG.* Kriminalpolitische Zeitschrift – Junges Publizieren, 15 with further sources.

20 In the original on p. 68: Wir führen die kontrollierte Abgabe von Cannabis an Erwachsene zu Genusszwecken in lizenzierten Geschäften ein. The coalition agreement can be found here. https://www.spd.de/fileadmin/Dokumente/Koalitionsvertrag/Koalitionsvertrag_2021-2025.pdf.

21 BVerfG, Beschluss der 3. Kammer des Zweiten Senats vom 5. Juli 2023 – 2 BvL 9/23, 2 BvL 15/23, 2 BvL 14/23, 2 BvL 11/23, 2 BvL 10/23 – lit 26.

The German Criminal Policy Debate on Cannabis

The criminal policy debate in Germany in the run-up to the decriminalization of cannabis revolved around three main aspects: How effective is the prohibition of cannabis, especially with regard to the already overburdened criminal justice system? How much of a deterrent effect does cannabis prohibition have on users? And could the existing black market for cannabis be effectively curbed by regulating the soft drug? These questions are not specific to Germany and have been the subject of international academic debate for many years. However, with regard to some specific features of the German criminal justice system, these questions are of particular relevance and will therefore be analyzed in more detail in the following.

First of all, it should be noted that the question of efficient criminal prosecution and a deterrent effect are more closely linked than might appear at first glance. With regard to the question of the deterring effects of cannabis prohibition, the argument in favor of regulation is rather straightforward: Prohibition has not worked since the number of consumers has been rising, not decreasing, as data on prevalence suggest. This argument, although compelling, is too simplistic. Indeed, deterrence is one of the most controversial issues in criminology and legal criminal research.[22] While deterrence and its effectiveness and impact on crime rates have been fiercely debated ever since this is not the place to add to this controversy. One argument that is often put forward by prohibitionists is that deterrence can only work if the laws are actually enforced. More specifically, with a view to cannabis, it can be argued that rising consumption is correlated with crime policies becoming increasingly lenient when it comes to enforcing the law. If prohibition is only on paper and, in reality, consumers and dealers remain unpunished, a deterrent effect might not occur. Hence, in view of the German debate, the question arises: How effectively has cannabis prohibition been implemented?

Probably, the best illustration to understand the answer to this question is a case example often used in German first-year criminal law courses to demonstrate the rather unique implications of German cannabis prohibition and its deep relation with criminal legal doctrine. The example goes as follows: If a person sits in a park with a couple of friends smoking a joint, no law is broken as under German law until recently, the consumption of cannabis was allowed but not the possession or distribution of it. Hence, the moment the joint is passed from one person to another, this would qualify as the distribution of an illegal substance. And while it is perfectly fine to smoke a joint containing a gram of weed, people did get in trouble for having the same amount in their pockets – as this would qualify as illegal possession. While indeed,

22 Bernard, T. J., Snipes, J. B., Gerould, A. L., & Vold, G. B. (2016). *Vold's theoretical criminology* (7th ed., p. 41). Oxford University Press.

these nuanced distinctions seem rather unique, the deeper reasoning behind exempting consumption from criminal liability – an exemption applying to all drugs, not only cannabis – is based on the simple assumptions that consumers should not be criminalized. Moreover, consuming, in essence, is equivalent to destroying the drug or, put differently, only a destroyed drug is good drug.

Empirical Data on Crimes Involving Cannabis

Besides these doctrinal and, in essence, anecdotal considerations, more telling is the empirical data on drug offenses collected by the German Federal Police Office annually. The official crime statistics of Germany register a total of over 340,677 narcotics offenses for the year 2022. Most of these, namely over 206,000 offenses (and thus around 60%), were related to cannabis.[23] Within this sub-group of cannabis-related offenses, one further distinguishes by the gravity of the offense. It makes a difference whether someone is caught with a few grams of cannabis in the pocket for personal consumption or with an entire truckload for large-scale black-market trade. However, in crime statistics, both offenses are recorded as one offense each. In order to paint a more precise picture of prohibition, German crime statistics include the category of 'consumption-related offenses' (*konsumnahe Delikte*). These are offenses that only include the possession, acquisition, and distribution of narcotics for personal use and not, for example, trafficking, cultivation, and possession of large quantities of cannabis, i.e., offenses that dealers and organized criminals typically commit. The consumption-related offenses in connection with cannabis still amount to about 175,000. This means that as many as 85% of the recorded cannabis-related offenses involved people who handled small amounts of the drug mainly for personal use.

These numbers are often used by legalization advocates to illustrate that prohibitions especially target consumers with very little criminal energy. While this may be true, one has to take these numbers with a pinch of salt. These numbers alone tell us little about how punitive German drug prohibition really is. If one considers that an estimated 200,000 joints are smoked *per day in* Germany, and more than 4.5 million people have consumed cannabis in the past 12 months (nearly half of them have consumed during the past 30 days), the annual amount of registered offenses seems rather moderate.[24] A similar situation can be observed in the United States, whose legal system is well known for being notoriously punitive, and where Caulkins et al. report

23 Bundeskriminalamt: Rauschgiftkriminalität Bundeslagebild 2020, 21.

24 Hoch, E., Olderbak, S., Schwarzkopf, L., Gomes de Matos, E., Schneider, F., & Deutsche Hauptstelle für Suchtfragen. (2024). Cannabis – Zahlen und Fakten. In *Deutsche Hauptstelle für Suchtfragen: Jahrbuch sucht 2024* (p. 93). Pabst.

less than 2% of users were actually arrested for possession in the course of an average year (between 2007 and 2013).[25]

Moreover, registered offenses are not to be confused with the crimes that are sentenced by criminal courts. Many of these registered offenses may not even go to trial or have any legal consequences for the offenders at all.[26] The reasons are partly based on the fact that German crime statistics only record the offenses registered by the police, i.e., those that have come to the attention of law enforcement. That means that for the German police, a case is considered solved as soon as a suspect can be assigned to an offense with sufficient probability. From there, the public prosecutor takes over and decides if the evidence is sufficient for an indictment or not. We will later see why this practice might be important when assessing the effectiveness of drug prohibition.

However, of utmost importance when putting these numbers of offenses in perspective is the fact that it is established case law of the German Federal Court that an amount of up to 6 grams of cannabis or a so-called small amount (*geringe Menge*) can be left unpunished by the courts.[27] Hence, law enforcement agencies can refrain from prosecuting these offenses. The emphasis is on 'can' – because they do not have to. This has led to the fact that prosecution for possession of cannabis was and is handled very differently in the German states. While in southern Germany, the possession of 2 grams could have led to criminal proceedings, the Berlin prosecution was more lenient and turned a blind eye to up to 15 grams of the soft drug.[28]

Enforcing Cannabis Prohibition in Germany

At first glance, this practice seems advantageous for consumers and surprisingly flexible for the notoriously formalistic German judicial system to exclude small amounts for personal use from punishment. Unfortunately, it is more complicated as the police still have to report all consumers, no matter the amount of cannabis. This is due to the principle of legality, a rather peculiar principle deeply rooted in German doctrinal thinking. In essence, this compels the German law enforcement authorities to prosecute every criminal offense that comes to their attention. The principle goes back far into the 19th century to one of the most prominent German legal scholars, Feuerbach, who

25 Caulkins et al., 2016, 95.

26 See for the problem of the attrition rate Walklate, S. (2016). Chapter 2: Counting crime. In *Criminology: The basics* (pp. 31–52). Taylor & Francis.

27 See § 29a V BtMG and the already cited Constitutional Court Decision where this practice is explained, BVerfG 90, 145, 9 March 1994, lit 165.

28 Deutscher Bundestag. *Legalisierung von Drogen in den Ländern der Europäischen Union und in der Schweiz* (p. 8). https://www.bundestag.de/resource/blob/411848/0f5bced02952c7a8be4d9f372ab06c49/wd-9-201-10-pdf-data.pdf.

thus shaped the German understanding of the rule of law.[29] It is based on the idea that the law equally applies to everyone and that the police cannot turn a blind eye to certain offenses or be granted any discretion when it comes to enforcing the law. Even more so, officers who do not investigate can even be liable to prosecution for obstruction of justice under Section 258 a of the Criminal Code.

It was already mentioned that the German judicial system has a tendency towards formalism, and the legality principle is a good illustration of this.[30] In reality, of course, not every offense that comes to the attention of the police is persecuted, but a report is filed and forwarded to the public prosecutor, who will then send the suspect a discontinuation notice. Hence in many cases involving small amounts of cannabis, this ultimately means that charges are dropped against consumers. However, since German criminal justice is notoriously overburdened, this may take a couple of months or even longer, leaving many consumers in the limbo of facing criminal charges. And one should not forget: A discontinuation is not an acquittal. It does not establish innocence, but it merely means that the criminal prosecution is terminated.[31]

It remains the question of whether the German prosecution service actually drops charges in cases involving small amounts of cannabis. As already mentioned, this strongly depends on where you are in Germany. Generally speaking, criminal justice is somewhat stricter in the south than in the north. A very rough picture can be deducted from the nationwide data published by the public prosecutor's offices, which show that in 2021 about 80,000 cases were discontinued based on § 31a BtMG.[32] If one assumes that the majority of the discontinuations relate to the soft drug cannabis and consumption-related offenses, then about 45% of all proceedings are discontinued, or almost half of all proceedings. While this might be good news for German cannabis consumers, it also drastically illustrates the inefficiency of cannabis prohibition. Before a case can be dropped, the police need to investigate, interrogate defendants and witnesses, and file a report, which is submitted to the prosecution service, where again, a public prosecutor needs to evaluate the prospects of going to trial and decide whether charges are pressed or not. This bureaucratic effort takes up a lot of time and resources, even more so if defense lawyers get involved.

29 Feuerbach, F. (1801). *Lehrbuch des gemeinen in Deutschland geltenden peinlichen Rechts*, *Heyer*.

30 Hofmann, R. (2022). Formalism versus pragmatism – a comparative legal and empirical analysis of the German and Dutch criminal justice systems with regard to effectiveness and efficiency. *Maastricht Journal of European and Comparative Law*, 28(4), 452–478.

31 This was regulated in §31a BtMG: according to this, the public prosecutor's office can discontinue the proceedings in cases of minor guilt or if the offender only cultivates, imports, or possesses the narcotics in small quantities for personal use.

32 StatistischesBundesamt.(2021).*RechtspflegeStaatsanwaltschaften–Fachserie10reihe2.6*(p.27). https://www.destatis.de/DE/Themen/Staat/Justiz-Rechtspflege/_inhalt.html#_4d6k8237o.

Now it becomes clear why many German justice officials, judges' associations, and police unions have called for a regulation of cannabis for years. The fact that their voices have been left unheard only until recently has led some to suspect that there might be systemic reasons besides sheer formalism for this inefficient approach. One of these reasons is probably to be found in the so-called crime clearance rates of the police. It was already mentioned that the police consider a case cleared whenever a suspect can be identified for a crime with a certain probability. The many small drug offenses, especially involving cannabis, have a very positive effect on the clearance rate of the police as the suspect is often known, easy to comprehend, and likely to confess.

The Black Market for Cannabis

An important criminological argument for the legalization of cannabis is the hope that it will make the illegal black market disappear. The logic behind this is simple: If you can get cannabis legally in a shop, you don't need to go to the dealer on the corner. The dealers will lose their business and so will the many cannabis growers who cultivate the plants in attics or remote greenhouses. Not to mention the smugglers who bring the cannabis herb or resin from North Africa, Turkey, the Netherlands, or Albania across the borders to Germany. In short, the criminal networks that currently have a firm grip on the German cannabis market would disappear. It would be a slow death, displaced by the forces of the free market, by the many legal cannabis providers and start-ups that can offer consumers a safer, better, and cheaper product. Even better: These companies not only create jobs but pay taxes. According to a much-cited study by the Heinrich Heine University in Düsseldorf, the total demand for cannabis in Germany is estimated at about 400 tons per year. If one sets the average price of 1 gram of cannabis at 10 euros, this results in a market volume of 4 billion euros. Economists estimate that more than half of this amount, i.e., 2.8 billion euros, would end up in the treasury through various taxes, such as a cannabis tax (similar to alcohol or tobacco tax), sales tax, or trade and corporate income tax. In addition, the state could save considerable costs. According to the study, in the case of the police alone, potential savings would amount to well over 1.36 billion euros, since thousands of investigations into the possession of small amounts of cannabis will be redundant. Added to this are several hundred million euros for public prosecutors, courts, and prisons, so the total amount that the state could realize through legalization amounts to about 4.7 billion euros.[33]

33 Haucap, J., & Knoke, L. (2021). *Fiskalische Auswirkungen Einer Cannabislegalisierung in Deutschland: Ein update.* https://www.dice.hhu.de/en/startseitennews/studie-cannabislegalisierung-bringt-dem-staat-jaehrlich-47-milliarden-euro-rund-27000-legale-arbeitsplaetze-wuerden-entstehen.

In the end, the only winners would be consumers, businesses, the state, and society. Organized crime, dealers, and smugglers would lose out. The question remains: How realistic is this scenario?

The Dynamics of Drug Markets

Black markets for drugs, including cannabis, follow their own complex dynamics. Criminologists and economists alike have been researching these dynamics in drug markets around the world for decades.[34] It is a fascinating topic because these black markets often show astonishing similarities to legal ones. The same free-market principles and displacement mechanisms apply, for example, through innovation and pricing. However, there are also a number of very significant differences. The most important from a criminological perspective is clearly the conflict resolution mechanisms, which vary greatly in drug markets.

Wherever people trade, conflicts arise. It is characteristic of civilized markets to resolve these conflicts effectively, ideally without the use of violence. Different mechanisms have developed for this worldwide, with complex legal systems, extensive commercial laws, specialized courts, and large law firms with thousands of lawyers who ensure that their clients emerge from a legal dispute as favorably as possible. This system is closed off to illicit players. For example, two German drug dealers who disagree about, say, the agreed quantity or quality of a shipment of cannabis don't have the option to take the matter before the commercial chamber of a district court. Neither would the court admit the matter for trial, but most likely, it would spark the interest of the public prosecutor's office. The fact that legal recourse is cut off does not automatically mean that conflicts in the drug business are always solved in a bloody way – just as it does not mean that all conflicts in the legal markets take place without violence. The actors in drug markets also have various informal instruments of conflict resolution at their disposal.

Nevertheless, violence and intimidation often play an important role in illegal markets. That is why firearms are so often seized when drugs are found. A Wild West mentality and the law of the strongest prevail. This results in a number of specific market dynamics that are difficult to fit into economists' model calculations. The seizure of a container of cocaine in the port of Rotterdam can have a direct impact on drug prices in Düsseldorf or Frankfurt. An escalating feud between two hostile mafia families in northern Italy can lead to a shortage of heroin in Berlin. The fact that South American cartels are increasingly pushing into the European market and displacing former players may trigger a reorganization of the entire market.[35]

34 See for an overview Ritter, A. (2006). Studying illicit drug markets: Disciplinary contributions. *International Journal of Drug Policy*, 17(6), 453–463.

35 Bundeskriminalamt: Rauschgiftkriminalität Bundeslagebild 2020, 23.

In addition, an upheaval has taken place on the drug markets in recent years: The darknet and the possibility to get drugs conveniently and with little risk via the internet has not only produced new groups of consumers. A completely new type of drug dealer has emerged who organizes the business from the computer at home and puts the old established street dealer networks under pressure. Especially during the coronavirus pandemic and the lockdowns, drug ordering online and mail and parcel delivery enjoyed great popularity. In 2020, the German Federal Police Office (BKA) identified 39 such online marketplaces with a connection to Germany alone – i.e., in Germany or with a shipping option to Germany.[36]

According to the BKA's drug report, the cannabis sold in Germany usually comes from indoor cultivation in Western Europe (including Belgium, Germany, the Netherlands, and Spain) but also from outdoor cultivation in Albania.[37] Overland, mostly by truck, the cannabis reaches Germany via the largely open borders, where it ends up on the black market, a misleading term as in fact, there is not one German black market but thousands of small, highly localized ones controlled by different players.

In criminological research, a distinction is made between three different cannabis black market types: The open, semi-open, and closed black market.[38] Open markets are mostly street markets that are open to all buyers, without special access barriers or the requirement to know the seller. Often, such black markets are aimed at tourists and can be well observed in big cities like Berlin or Amsterdam. In closed markets, on the other hand, social relations between dealers and buyers are crucial as business is based on mutual trust. New customers are acquired through recommendations from already established customers. Semi-open black markets operate in places like clubs and cafés, and while the supply of cannabis does not require prior social relationships, consumers need to know where the black market is located and have access to it. In Germany, all three types of black market exist, without it being possible to clearly state which type dominates and where.

What Will Happen to the Black Market After Legalization?

With this complex structure of the German cannabis market in mind, one can only speculate if legalization will really result in a curbing of the black market. Despite many advocates of legalization vehemently claiming this with plausible argument, a scientifically sound prognosis on this would require a

36 Bundeskriminalamt: Rauschgiftkriminalität Bundeslagebild 2020, 13.

37 Bundeskriminalamt: Rauschgiftkriminalität Bundeslagebild 2020, 14.

38 Skliamis, K., & Korf, D. (2022). How cannabis users obtain and purchase cannabis: A comparison of cannabis users from European countries with different cannabis policies. *Substance Use & Misuse*, 57(7), 1043–1051. https://doi.org/10.1080/10826084.2022.2058707.

criminological crystal ball. Empirical studies on black-market dynamics after legalization are rare and are based on models and assumptions rather than collected data. This is not surprising, as only very few countries have legalized cannabis so far, and studies on the influence on the black markets there are methodologically very complex. For example, initial studies from Canada show that there, despite legalization, a considerable amount of cannabis is still bought on the black market and especially on the internet, even after several years.[39] But to deduce from this that legalization has no or only minor effects on the black market and to apply this data to Germany is ill-advised. Canada is a large country, and many consumers live in the countryside. Since most shops are located in big cities, postal delivery plays an important role, and since legal cannabis is not available via delivery, the black market still plays a significant role. Also, prices for legal cannabis could not keep up with the black market prices either, so many consumers, especially poorer ones, continue to rely on black-market cannabis. The study even suggests that the relationship of Canadians to their dealer might play a role: Once you have found a good dealer, you stick with him, despite legal options being available.[40]

These results from Canada are not easily transferable to Germany. As already mentioned, Drug markets are often locally characterized. Contrary to Canada, Germany is densely populated, and hence, the online market might play a smaller role. Nevertheless, experiences from other countries can provide important clues as to how legalization should be designed in order to displace the black market effectively. For example, pricing plays an important role: Legal cannabis must not be significantly more expensive than black-market cannabis, as otherwise, users will continue to resort to black-market cannabis. This means that the state must not only keep an eye on the tax burden of cultivators. It also must consider intervening if the price of cannabis suddenly rises, for example, if energy costs explode and the production of indoor cannabis becomes more expensive. Moreover, legal cannabis must also not be significantly cheaper than that available on the black market as this bears the chance of dealers stocking up on legal cannabis and selling it at a profit on the black market.

In summary, predictions about the development of the cannabis black market in the wake of legalization are difficult to make. Although a reduction and curbing of the black market seem plausible, there is a lack of scientific evidence to support this assumption. Much will depend on how the regulations are conceptualized and how consumers react to the new situation. What is clear is the fact that it will take time until positive effects can be measured.

39 Noonan, N. (2021). High time for change: Combatting the black market for cannabis in Canada. *Manitoba Law Journal*, 44(3), 257–297.

40 Noonan, 2021, 259.

Conclusion

After analyzing the scientific literature, it seems that criminologists are largely in agreement: The criminalization of cannabis does more harm than good.[41] Especially in the US debate, it is not only the overburdening of the justice system but also the overcrowding of prisons, as well as racial discrimination, that play a role in the prosecution of cannabis offenses.[42] Health-related issues, youth protection, and black-market dynamics have been widely debated in Germany. It shows how complex the debate on cannabis is, and those looking for simple arguments and justifications will be disappointed. This might also explain why both supporters and opponents of legalization argue their point of view with almost religious zeal. The pro-legalization advocates want to make people understand that smoking pot is a human right and that prohibition is not only ineffective but inevitably leads to crime, discrimination, and death. Opponents, on the other hand, with their 'resist the beginnings' mentality, see the direct path to societal demise at even a millimeter's distance from the strict prohibition policy. Both views are exaggerated; the truth, as so often, lies somewhere in between. But where exactly?

This chapter has shown that there is undoubtedly a lot to be said in favor of legalizing cannabis.

In the long run, it is likely that the black market will shrink. Organized criminal networks will lose profits. But how will they react to this? Flood the market with harder drugs at cheaper prices? Then legalization could have detrimental effects, and freed law enforcement capacities must be used against the hard drugs. The protection of minors remains a contradiction that cannot be easily solved: They remain excluded from the legal supply even though this demographic is the most vulnerable to the negative effects of black-market cannabis, including health damage from contaminated or highly potent cannabis. Moreover, they are particularly easily influenced by black-market dealers. Consequently, controlled distribution to young people should be allowed. But a state that supplies its young people with cannabis? Hard to imagine. After all, you can't have everything: Legalization cannot solve all problems. Those who have too high expectations can easily be disappointed.

41 Caulkins et al., 2016, 22. In the US this growing consensus dates back to the early '70s with the publication of influential books on the issue.

42 Firth, C. L., Hajat, A., Dilley, J. A., Braun, M., & Maher, J. E. (2020). Preventing substance use disorders in young people: A review of the effectiveness of prevention strategies. *American Journal of Preventive Medicine*, 58(4), 562–569.

3 The International Prohibition of Cannabis

Introduction

In most countries around the world, cannabis is a forbidden substance. Almost all countries are parties to a tightly knit system of so-called drug control treaties. These treaties are like a prohibitionist bulwark that has known only one premise for almost a century: The prohibition of all psychotropic substances, i.e., all drugs, including cannabis. Exceptions apply only for scientific and medical purposes. 'Medical purposes' refers to the many different uses of substances in medicine, such as opiates for pain therapy or synthetic drugs for treating anxiety disorders. The use of drugs for scientific purposes comprises the testing and experimenting with prohibited substances, for example, to develop new medical drugs or to treat addiction. Indeed, many drugs can be used for medical purposes in one way or another or have broader scientific use. International law, therefore, rightfully allows these exceptions. This, however, does not change the fact that drugs for recreational use are generally prohibited.

But why did some countries voluntarily curb their sovereignty to determine which drugs to allow and which to prohibit by placing themselves under a strict international control regime? And why have so many countries remained within this system even when domestic drug policies have changed towards more liberal approaches? Is there any leeway or a legal loophole within this control regime for signatory states to regulate cannabis without breaching the treaties? Is it possible at all to legalize cannabis in compliance with international law? The legal debate about these questions has been going on for decades.[1] Legalization advocates argue that the prohibitionist system is obsolete and does indeed offer room for change. Sometimes their

1 See for example Room, R., Fischer, B., Hall, W., Lenton, S., & Reuter, P. (2010). *Cannabis policy: Moving beyond Stalemate*. Brickley Foundation; Van Kempen, P. H., & Federova, M. (2019). *International law and cannabis: Regulation of cannabis cultivation for recreational use under the UN narcotic drugs conventions and the EU legal instruments in anti-drugs policy*. Intersentia.

DOI: 10.4324/9781003503439-4

arguments are convincing; sometimes, creativity in interpreting the regulations seems to trump reason. And all too often, their interpretations amount to wishful thinking, driven by the understandable but not very realistic desire for a fundamental and far-reaching reform of the prohibitionist drug control regime.

Not surprisingly, their arguments have remained unheard, and the treaty regime has been left unchanged. But recently, the unlikely has happened, and something has started to move in the debate. This change was triggered by Bolivia, a South American country caught in the eye of the storm of the international war on drugs for years. Although Bolivia's endeavor was directed toward regulating the chewing of coca leaves, it poured new fuel into the debate about legalizing cannabis. Some countries like Canada and Uruguay have skipped this debate entirely by legalizing cannabis. But in doing so, they deliberately broke international law. Other countries like the Netherlands and Germany took the chance to revisit their standpoint on cannabis and explore new possibilities for their drug policies. Especially in Germany, the legal debate gained momentum, culminating in the summer of 2021 with the new German government putting full legalization of cannabis on the political agenda. Until then, the legalization debate had been dominated by a few legal scholars and legalization activists but was followed by a controversial debate and numerous legal opinions about the feasibility of government plans. At the core of the dispute was compliance of the plans with international and European law.

In this chapter, we will trace some of the most important lines of argumentation of the advocates of legalization as well as the opponents. The focus will be on the German debate for several reasons. German criminal law and jurisprudence look back on a long tradition of doctrinal thinking. Hence, legislative projects like the (partial) legalization of cannabis, which deeply reaches into criminal law and crime policies, requires a solid legal foundation. A trial by error or approach of deregulating first and providing the legal framework later was never an option. Contrary to other countries that have legalized cannabis, the German approach was, from the beginning, very formalistic and driven by the ambition to comply with international rules. While different legal strategies on how to achieve cannabis regulation in compliance with international law have been discussed for years, many of these have been developed in the echo chambers of a tightly knitted expert community streamlined by the common denominator that reforming the drug treaty system is inevitable. The government plans in Germany not only prompted a number of legal assessments and opinions from more objective experts but also required political and legal feasibility instead of idealism. Some main aspects of this debate will be outlined as these provide valuable insights for other states toying with the idea of legalizing cannabis – both as a legal blueprint and as an example of which mistakes, detours, and dead ends to avoid.

The Control Illusion of International Law

Admittedly, the legal debate about regulating drugs is complex. But there are good reasons for this: It deals with significant issues like public health, crime prevention, entire states corrupted by drug trafficking, centuries-old consumption practices deeply rooted in indigenous cultures, human rights, half a century of 'War on Drugs', and last but not least with commercial interests. The global drug trade is highly lucrative. For some, it promises fabulous riches while for most of those involved, the drug trade means exploitation and violence.

The international rules, which almost all states in the world have accepted, operate in these areas of tension. While many details of the drug control regime may be disputable, the fact that there is a global consensus on prohibiting drugs is somewhat impressive. This, perhaps, is the first thing to realize if one wants to understand the dynamics of the drug control regime: There is a difference between the law on paper and its enforcement. The fact that drug use is more widespread today than ever before and that drug trafficking is more prolific and lucrative than ever in world history is not due to a lack of consensus among the international community. Instead, two main reasons play a role. First, there is a classic problem of criminal law: A prohibition is not worth the paper it is written on if it is not also enforced by state power. Many states profit massively from drug trafficking. Consequently, they have little interest in taking effective measures against it, although they would be obliged to do so.

The second reason is a classic criminological problem: The drug control regime is based on the idea that crime phenomena can be curbed or even made to disappear if only strict laws are imposed and sufficient resources are devoted to controlling, enforcing, and fighting them. This is an illusion, a control illusion, to be precise. As far as the international drug trade is concerned, we have long since lost control – this is if we ever possessed it in the first place. Arguably, we never had real control over drug use and trafficking, not to speak over the organized criminals that profit from it. The idea that social problems can be solved through criminal law is deeply rooted in our understanding of the rule of law. These things must be considered if one wants to understand the *status quo* of international law on drug control and trafficking. The treaty regime has solidified like a fossil over the years: Adjustments to new scientific findings, political processes, and the liberal *zeitgeist* have passed it by. If one wanted to adapt the treaties, it would require the consent of a majority or all contracting parties, i.e., the world's nations, and a consensus on a controversial and highly politicized issue like drug control is not in sight.

Despite all this, international law and, even more so, European law affect the possibilities of cannabis legalization in the contracting states. Germany is a sovereign state and can, in principle, determine for itself how it shapes laws, what is permitted, and what is prohibited. However, international rules limit this sovereignty. Decades ago, Germany committed itself contractually – through the international drug control treaties or the EU treaties – to abide by specific rules. These rules bind today's government. It cannot claim that certain agreements are no longer valid because they date back to the previous government's time. If the current government does not agree with these rules, it can, of course, terminate the agreements if it wants to. But can it also terminate only those regulations that do not suit it at the moment (for example, the ban on cannabis) but otherwise remain a party to the agreement? In other words, could it pick cherries, opting in for the rules and regulations that benefit its interest while abandoning those that don't? This, indeed, is one of the crucial questions this chapter will deal with.

The Problem With the Global Drug Trade

International law regulates relations between states and between states and international organizations. It comprises many international treaties, agreements, conventions, covenants, etc. International law regulates matters that have international relevance. Conversely, it does not regulate matters merely of national interest which fall exclusively within the sovereignty of nation-states. This should be made clear first, as there are often misunderstandings, especially regarding cannabis and other drugs. One could argue that drug policy falls solely within the competence of nation-states. After all, what is it to do with Morocco, for example, if cannabis for pain relief is available in pharmacies in Germany? What does France have to do with it if opium poppies are grown in Afghanistan for opium and, ultimately, heroin production?

Well, in the first case, it really is none of Morocco's business. From the point of view of international law, states are essentially free to decide how they shape their health policies. In the second case, it is not quite so simple. At first sight, the fact that Afghanistan is currently ravaged by a heroin epidemic, with thousands of people dying every year, is not the problem of France. The human tragedy behind it may well move the French. However, France as a nation or – to stay with the legal terminology – as a subject of international law does not directly influence this Afghan health problem. Indirectly, however, it does affect France as a considerable part of heroin sold on the French black market comes from Afghanistan. The drug trade is global. This is true not only for heroin but for almost every other drug imaginable. If Afghanistan were to destroy all opium poppy fields overnight, there would be fewer heroin deaths not only in Afghanistan but also in France. This is more or less the logic of the international control treaties.

A global community has a common interest in prohibiting drugs – or better, *preventing* them. Because the past has taught us that prohibition alone is not enough. According to this logic based on a public health approach, Afghanistan and France would both be better off if Afghanistan prevented the cultivation of opium poppies. This simplified view, however, disregards the dynamics of the global drug trade. This trade is entirely unregulated, meaning that no state authorities have any control over the distribution chain from cultivation and production to export and sale to the end user. It is widely unclear how large the quantity of drugs is in a given market, what the quality of the drugs is, and how the pricing works. Market participants, from drug cartels to street dealers, thus find themselves in an ideal market situation where no tariffs or government protection distort competition while profit margins are enormous. For example, experts estimate that it costs about 1,000 euros to produce a kilo of cocaine in South America, while it can easily make far over 50,000 euros on the European illicit market. Moreover, people addicted to drugs are ideal customers: If the pressure of addiction is only big enough, rational choices about supply and demand, quality, and price are barely made. All too often communities bear these negative consequences of drug markets, be it in the form of health or crime costs.

Not only have drugs the tendency to create costs far away from where they are produced. Another problem is that the drug trade is so lucrative that it has corrupted entire states. The state and economic elites in so-called narco-states make a good living from the drug trade. Narco-states are states whose political and economic elites are corrupted by the drug business.[2] The motivation to fight drug production and trade effectively is, to put it mildly, low in these states. Classic examples of narco-states can be found in South America, such as Bolivia, Honduras, and Mexico. But they also include Syria, whose regime finances the war against its population with the trade in the synthetic drug Captagon. It is currently being discussed whether the Netherlands should also be counted as a narco-state, a question which will be addressed in Chapter 5.

The international community has two options for action to combat international drug trafficking: On the one hand, one could regulate the trade, as is already done with tobacco and alcohol, which would require legalizing drugs. The second option is to destroy the black market following the logic that where there are no drugs, there are no consumers and thus no adverse consequences. While both options are somewhat simplified, it seems the world community has opted for the second option. The successes of this approach have been somewhat limited so far, to say the least. However, this is not because of disagreement on the matter or its necessity. The problem lies instead in the enforcement of the strict prohibition regime. Not only is there a lack of resources, but there also is a lack of will on the part of some states. Why should a poor country like Bolivia put massive resources into fighting cocaine production and trafficking when most of it ends up with wealthy Wall Street bankers who can't get enough of it? Wouldn't it be up to the USA to limit demand, for example, through education campaigns or by punishing

2 Hofmann, R. (2021). Is the Netherlands a narco-state? *Der Kriminalist*, 2021(12).

consumption? Couldn't this be a third option in the fight against the global drug trade, starting with the consumers and curbing their consumption? If we were to consistently educate people about the harmfulness of drugs, the related health risks, the dangers of addiction, the social costs, and the disruptive dynamics that the poorest countries of the world have to bear, no one would take drugs anymore. Where there is no demand for drugs, there is no supply and, consequently, no drug markets. Unfortunately, it is not that simple.

Reducing the demand for drugs is a sore point in the fight against drugs. Reducing demand is a lengthy and expensive endeavor with an unknown outcome. For example, one of the most extensive drug education programs in world history, the DARE program, was shut down in the US after years and billions of dollars invested because it simply had little effect. On the contrary, studies have shown that drug education in schools often has the adverse effect of creating an interest in drugs among students in the first place. Drug consumption has only ever gone in one direction: Upwards. It fluctuates from time to time; sometimes, various drugs are more popular, and sometimes, less. Overall, however, we see an increase in all major types of drugs in almost all countries around the world.[3]

International Law and Drugs

The fact that the current control regime has not reduced drugs but, contrary, seems to have increased production and consumption is often taken as evidence that prohibition has failed. Indeed, this might be the strongest and most repeated argument voiced by those advocating for legalizing cannabis or other drugs. While this argument is plausible in many respects, the conclusion drawn that regulating drugs is the only viable path forward is far from compelling. Maybe the prohibitionist system might be flawed and just has to be revised to be more effective. Maybe the legal regime is functioning okay, but the implementation by the treaty states lacks determination. Maybe without global drug prohibition, the situation would be even grimmer, with more drug-related crimes and deaths and addiction soaring to unknown heights. This or something similar is the sound of the counter-arguments brought against legalization or regulation initiatives. No matter how one positions oneself on the issue, to make an informed decision, it is worth having a closer look at the treaties and those provisions that keep prohibition afloat.

Indeed, the fact that consumption has been increasing for decades is also why we are not dealing with one international drug control treaty but with three. The Single Convention of 1961 united nine conventions and was

3 See the UNODC. (2022). *World drug report 2022, drug market trends cannabis opiods*. UNODC.

supposed to simplify and standardize drug prohibition (hence Single Convention). Only ten years later, the use of LSD, in particular, had increased so much that it was decided to supplement the Single Convention with the Convention on Psychotropic Substances. Then, a few years later, a further step was deemed necessary. In 1988, the world community agreed on the United Nations Convention against Illicit Traffic in Narcotic Drugs and Psychotropic Substances. The Convention aims primarily at improving international cooperation against drug trafficking.

Regarding the possibilities of cannabis legalization under international law, it is essential to be clear about one central aspect of these conventions: The obligations in the conventions require the proactiveness of the signing parties. This means they do not only contain obligations to criminalize trafficking or trade in specific drugs formally. Instead, the signatory states are obliged to prevent this trade proactively. After all, what good are the strictest criminal laws if the state does not enforce them? National criminal justice systems can give law enforcement agencies considerable leeway in deciding how and which offenses they prosecute. When it comes to drugs, however, this leeway exists only to a minimal extent, as the drug control treaties make clear in many provisions. This also has consequences for the cannabis policies of the signatory states.

The Relevant Norms

Let us first take a look at the drug control treaties, starting with the Single Convention of 1961 where Article 36(1) states:

> *Subject to its constitutional limitations, each Party shall adopt such measures as will ensure that cultivation, production, manufacture, extraction, preparation, possession, offering, offering for sale, distribution, purchase, sale, delivery on any terms whatsoever, brokerage, dispatch, dispatch in transit, transport, importation and exportation of drugs . . . punishable offences when committed intentionally, and that serious offences shall be liable to adequate punishment particularly by imprisonment or other penalties of deprivation of liberty.*

That cannabis in any form falls under these prohibited narcotic substances follows from Article 1 of the Convention. The exaggerated listing of prohibited behavior shows how important it was to the signatory states to leave no loopholes. The difference between 'distribution', 'transport', or 'important/export' may in reality be marginal but apparently creators wanted to be on the safe side.

Article 4c then contains a significant exception to the prohibition. There, States Parties are obliged to limit: 'production, manufacture, export, import, distribution of, trade in, use and possession of drugs' exclusively to medical and scientific purposes. This is the crucial exception for scientific and medical purposes already mentioned. Because of this exception, the state parties are explicitly allowed to regulate trade in medicinal cannabis and opioids as medicines.

Article 5 of the 1971 Convention on Narcotic Drugs reiterates and emphasizes this restriction for medical and scientific purposes. Then, 17 years later, in the United Nations Convention against Illicit Traffic in Narcotic Drugs and Psychotropic Substances of 1988, the prohibition of cannabis is again specified and emphasized. Article 3a) ii explicitly states that the contracting parties undertake to define as criminal offenses 'the cultivation . . . of the cannabis plant for the purpose of the production of narcotic drugs contrary to the provisions of the 1961 Convention'.

However, this 1988 agreement differs from the Single Convention in one crucial point: As the agreement is designed to combat global drug trafficking Article 3(2) contains the following provision:

> *Subject to its constitutional principles and the basic concepts of its legal system, each Party shall adopt such measures as may be necessary to establish as a criminal offence under its domestic law, when committed intentionally, the possession, purchase or cultivation of narcotic drugs or psychotropic substances for personal consumption contrary to the provisions of the 1961 Convention, the 1961 Convention as amended or the 1971 Convention.*

This wording of the provision, and especially the condition of subjecting the measures taken to establish criminal offenses to constitutional principles, is interpreted in the way that it allows signatory states to decriminalize cannabis possession for personal consumption.

Incidentally, the 1988 Convention contains a whole series of provisions on the punishment of drug possession and trafficking, which should not be of further interest here. What is clear, however, is that the treaties are pretty clear on criminalizing drugs in general and cannabis in particular. To get an idea of how solemn these treaties are about drug prohibition, a look at the preamble of the 1988 agreement is telling: Deep concerns are expressed by the 'increasing inroads into various social groups made by illicit traffic in narcotic drugs and psychotropic substances, and particularly by the fact that children are used in many parts of the world as an illicit drug consumers market'. Psychotropic substances are considered to entail 'dangers of incalculable gravity', and drug trafficking is linked to 'organized criminal activities which undermine the legitimate economies and threaten the stability, security, and sovereignty of States'.

After this brief look at just a few of the many provisions, the question remains: Where do legalization advocates see any leeway to legalize cannabis without breaching the treaties? How can signatory states like Germany set out to regulate the trade with cannabis, a psychotropic substance under the treaty definition, without violating international law with all its possible consequences?

Indeed, it seems puzzling, but in the German legalization debate a so-called interpretative declaration may be the sword to cut the gordian knot of international cannabis prohibition. After the German government had included the plan to fully legalize cannabis in its coalition agreement, it issued a concept paper in October 2022. There it stated:

> *Against this background, the Federal Government prefers the option of issuing an interpretative declaration to the other parties to the international conventions and the international drug control bodies, according to which it declares this implementation of the coalition agreement . . . to be compatible with the purpose and legal requirements of the conventions.*

In other words, Germany just declares to all other signatory parties that it interprets the international treaties in the way that these allow full legalization of cannabis. At first sight, this approach seems puzzling as treaty obligations tend not to disappear into thin air by a simple declaration along the lines of: We recognize the prohibition but just interpret the wording of the regulations in the exact opposite way. However, on closer inspection, there is more to this approach.

The German Interpretation Declaration

In theory, the interpretation declaration is a legally complex but clever instrument to achieve the legalization of cannabis in compliance with international drug control treaties. Interestingly enough, it received rather little attention in the academic literature, probably because of its complexity and deep rooting in German doctrinal thinking. To understand the thought behind it, one has to dig deep into the UN Convention of 1988 and go to its very end, where declarations and reservations can be found. Whereas the latter will be an issue we deal with at a later stage, for now, the declarations are of interest. These are sometimes made by states when signing treaties in order to clarify their understanding of a specific matter or interpretation of a provision.[4] Declarations are made to clarify the positions of the signatory state but do not modify the legal effect of the treaty and are not always legally binding. Germany made such a declaration back in 1989, and it reads as follows: ‘It is the understanding of the Federal Republic of Germany that the basic concepts of the legal system referred to in article 3, paragraph 2 of the Convention may be subject to change’.

4 See Glossary of terms relating to treaty actions available here. https://treaties.un.org/pages/overview.aspx?path=overview/glossary/page1_en.xml.

Article 3 was mentioned earlier: It constitutes the obligation to criminalize certain behaviors related to drugs. However, it also mentions constitutional principles and the exemption of personal consumption. In other words, Germany declared with the signing of the treaty that the obligation to criminalize certain behaviors related to drugs may change over time. But what does this exactly mean? And, more importantly, what follows from this?

The idea back then was to leave the door open for a possible decriminalization of cannabis at a later point in time.[5] While the declaration is formulated rather vaguely, leaving room for much interpretation, the details of what exactly constitutes this change may be of less relevance. The German government had left the door open back then for a different path in its cannabis policy, and now it's time to pass through that door. While this seems a rather formal justification, advocates of the interpretation declaration argue further by referring to the treaty's core. Their argument: The treaty's goals, i.e., the fighting of drug-related crimes and health protection, can only be achieved by legalizing cannabis.

We have already seen that cannabis is the most widely used drug in the world. Research today is further advanced than it was in the '50s and '60s. We know much better today how cannabis works, what health risks are associated with it, and how and whether it is addictive. At the same time, consumption has increased enormously in the last decades, and cannabis has become a lifestyle drug consumed mainly by young people. They depend on the vast black market, on dealers and organized criminals who are driven solely by greed for profit and who do not care about health risks. They cut the cannabis with potentially dangerous substances or sell it in a highly potent form to get kids hooked. If we want to achieve the goals of the drug control treaties – i.e., safety and health protection, especially for our children – we have to legalize cannabis and not ban it. In other words, to achieve the goals of the drug control treaties and to fulfill its obligations, Germany is not only allowed but even obliged to legalize the recreational use of cannabis.[6]

Two Problems of the Interpretation Declaration

While this argument seems plausible both in terms of the formal declaration included in the UN Convention and with regard to its broader scope and goals of the treaty, there are at least two problems connected to this reasoning: The first problem relates to the scope of Article 3, paragraph 2 of the Convention. The second problem relates to the European Union, which is also a signatory party of the Convention.

5 See Ambos, K. (2022). *Zur völkerrechtlichen Zulässigkeit der Cannabis-Entkriminalisierung*. Footnote 29. https://verfassungsblog.de/zur-volkerrechtlichen-zulassigkeit-der-cannabis-entkriminalisierung/.

6 A similar reasoning can be found here: Van Kempen & Federova, 2019, 230–231.

The first problem is a classical legal problem of interpreting the wording of a treaty obligation. Interestingly enough, here, it seems to be based on a common misunderstanding that has been surprisingly widespread in the debate about cannabis legalization. In simple terms, this misunderstanding is based on the assumption that if the personal use of cannabis is allowed, this must also include the possibility of obtaining small amounts of cannabis for personal use. After all, what good is it to allow cannabis for personal use if there are no legal sources to obtain this cannabis? These are the two sides of the same coin. However, treaties like the UN Convention are not always based on practicability or reason. Legalizing the personal use of cannabis without allowing the commercial trade is a possible solution – although maybe not the ideal one.

The wording of Article 3, paragraph 2, although a bit vague, allows the regulation of personal consumption of cannabis. This, however, does not include the production of cannabis to meet the demand of the consumers.

The advocates of the German interpretation declaration, which explicitly refers to Article 3, did, of course, see this problem and argue rather vaguely that the commercial trade is some sort of a natural correlate of personal use and that legalizing personal use by means of logic includes the legalization of production and supply.[7] From a legal point of view, this remains a bit of a stretch, to say the least. The personal use of cannabis and the large-scale production and supply of the same are two very different things. The fact that this is clearly reflected in the wording of the treaties cannot just be interpreted away.

Secondly, there is a more technical but also potentially more profound problem related to the declaration Germany gave in 1989. This issue was widely overlooked in the legal discussion about the German interpretation declaration.[8] It relates to the fact that the European Union as well had signed the UN convention in 1989 (at that time as the European Economic Community) but without a similar declaration. Germany is a member state of the European Union. So, the door left open for cannabis legalization by the German declaration might have been closed by the European Union accessing the convention. Even if Germany would waive its obligations from the convention and fully legalize cannabis, it would still be indirectly bound to the same obligations through the European Union. This was even further

7 See Wegener, B. (2023). *Völker- und europarechtliche Grenzen einer Cannabis-Legalisierung in Deutschland Rechtsgutachten für die Bayerische Staatsregierung* (p. 35). https://www.stmgp.bayern.de/wp-content/uploads/2023/03/gutachten_cannabis-legalisierung.pdf.

8 The problem was first addressed here by Hofmann, R. (2022). *Welche Probleme das Cannabiskontrollgesetz lösen muss – Deutschlands Cannabis-Dilemma Teil 2*. https://verfassungsblog.de/cannabis-2/. A later later more in depth analysis can be found here by Thym, D. (2022). *Ein Weg zur Cannabis-Legalisierung führt über Luxemburg*. https://verfassungsblog.de/ein-weg-zur-cannabis-legalisierung-fuhrt-uber-luxemburg/.

complicated by the fact that initially, the EEC only accessed a specific part of the convention due to the limited competencies it had back then. Meanwhile, the European Union, as the legal successor, has achieved these competencies but has never formally declared that it would fully access the convention. A legal opinion published by the German parliament deals extensively with this intricate legal problem but reaches no clear conclusion on the matter.[9] Despite the question of what this exactly means for Germany's (or any other EU member state's) ambitions to legalize cannabis, the fact that this problem was widely overlooked in the previous legal debate dampened the high hopes legalization advocates had put into the German solution of an interpretation declaration.

Alternatives to the Re-Interpretation of the Treaties

The cultivation, trade, and transfer of psychotropic substances is prohibited. The only exception is for medical and scientific purposes. These rules have been in place for well over half a century, since 1961, to be precise, and they apply worldwide: 183 states have signed the Single Convention. Germany considers this strict ban on cannabis to be outdated. Other signatory states have voiced a similar view. Like all treaties, drug control treaties could be amended to remove cannabis from the list of psychotropic substances. Then, each country could introduce its cannabis policy. In the case of the Single Convention, all the contracting states would have to agree to an amendment. How realistic would that be? The answer is sobering. There are very few countries in the world that openly consider the regulation of cannabis to be the right way to control its use. While their number might be growing, the discussion about changing the treaties has been of academic nature with little practical relevance.

One option would be to simply ignore the international treaties. This is what Canada and Uruguay have done. These two countries have signed the Single Convention and the two other drug control treaties. Nevertheless, both states fully legalized cannabis, Uruguay in 2013 and Canada in 2017. We will see later how exactly this was implemented and which challenges they encountered. The legal consequences, however, for the breach of international law were limited. Disputes arising from the conventions can be referred to the International Court of Justice in The Hague (ICJ). It may render a decision on the matter but has no enforcement power: You can hardly put a state in prison. The sharpest sword of the international community is sanctions. Neither Canada nor Uruguay have been sanctioned for breaching the drug control

9 Deutscher Bundestag. (2023). *Unionsrechtlich eröffnete Regelungsfreiheiten der Mitgliedstaaten im Bereich Cannabis*. Ausarbeitung EU 6-3000-024/23, 11. https://www.bundestag.de/resource/blob/959066/2bbc73133791ba5b6ea5bd26a1af6e44/EU-6-024-23-pdf-data.pdf.

treaties. International law is a toothless tiger. The system is based on trust that signatory states comply with the rules and that no force is needed.

Germany has embraced this somehow idealistic foundation of international law. The German constitution is *völkerrechtsfreundlich* (friendly to international law), meaning that compliance with international rules is a high priority. The reasons for this can be found in German history and the lessons learned from blatantly breaching international law during two world wars. This is also the reason why the path of deliberately ignoring the drug control treaties in order to legalize cannabis has never been a viable option for Germany.

A Reservation for Cannabis?

While ignoring the treaties is out of the question for Germany, an alternative route has dominated the legal debate about legalizing cannabis in compliance with international law for quite some time now.[10] The solution suggested for Germany lies in the inclusion of a reservation for cannabis in international treaties. What exactly is a reservation, and how does it work? Reservations are a bit like institutionalized cherry-picking in international law. While widely despised by legal scholars, these are regularly found in international treaties.[11] Reservations are exceptions to specific treaty regulations which apply to certain signatory states. More precisely, reservations are declarations made by states that purport to exclude or alter the legal effect of specific treaty provisions in their application to the state.[12]

Such reservations exist in drug control treaties, for example, in the UN Convention of 1988, in which Peru was granted a reservation for the chewing of coca leaves. Article 3(a)ii of the treaty expressly makes the illegal cultivation of coca bushes a punishable offense. Due to the reservation, this regulation does not apply to Peru as the country declared a reservation for the drug.[13] This prompts the question of why Peru joined the treaty if it was unwilling to fulfill its rules. Peru is one of the most important source countries for various drugs, but especially for cocaine. The coca bush thrives particularly well in the climate of the Andes. Having such a global player at the table is essential to establish an effective international drug policy. At the same time, coca leaves are the raw material from which cocaine is produced. Leaving the

10 See Room et al., 2010.

11 Helfer, L. R. (2006). Not fully committed reservations, risk, and treaty design. *Yale Journal of International Law*, 31(2), 367–382.

12 UN Glossary of terms relating to treaty action available here. https://treaties.un.org/pages/overview.aspx?path=overview/glossary/page1_en.xml#reservation.

13 More precisely, the reservation refers to the question of what is meant by illegal cultivation, since Peru considers the cultivation of coca leaves to be legal.

country out of the treaty regime would have been a significant loss for the world community. In that sense, the Peruvian reservation is a compromise that international law provides to encourage countries to accede to treaties in the first place. In that logic, a treaty with reservations is better than one that only a handful of countries have signed.

A second issue is essential when it comes to reservations in international law. In our example, Peru was granted a reservation for the chewing of coca leaves before signing the UN Convention of 1988. Generally, reservations can be made when the treaty is signed, ratified, accepted, approved, or acceded to.[14] But what if a state wants to include a reservation later, i.e., when the treaty has already been signed and ratified? This question was important for Germany's legalization plans for obvious reasons: The country did not include a reservation when signing the treaties. Formally, Germany would have to withdraw from the drug control treaties (denounce them) and accede again, this time with a reservation for cannabis. There is one precedent of a country successfully being granted a reservation retroactively: That country is Bolivia, and the reservation relates to the chewing of coca leaves.

Bolivia's Withdrawal and Re-Entry Into the Single Convention

Similar to Peru, chewing coca leaves is a tradition in Bolivia. The indigenous population, which mostly lives in the vast rural and jungle-covered areas of the country, indulges in this centuries-old custom. The leaves are picked directly from the coca bush and chewed or prepared as tea. Thousands of small farmers cultivate the shrub on their barren fields on bitterly poor farms. This is exactly what makes the matter so delicate: The primary purpose of chewing coca leaves is not to get high. In fact, the intoxicating effect of coca leaves has very little to do with cocaine intoxication. The production of cocaine is relatively complex and requires multiple ingredients, such as highly toxic chemicals and even diesel. Chewing coca leaves can suppress feelings of hunger, thirst, and pain.[15] These are essential properties for some of the poorest people in one of the most remote regions of the world.

Why should the indigenous be denied their age-old tradition? One could argue that Bolivia is one of the largest cocaine producers in the world. It is impossible to distinguish farms that grow coca bushes for chewing from coca grown for cocaine production. Only a general ban strictly enforced by

14 UN Glossary of terms relating to treaty action available here. https://treaties.un.org/pages/overview.aspx?path=overview/glossary/page1_en.xml#reservation.

15 Casanovas, M., Jiménez-Rosés, M., Cordomí, A., Lillo, A., Vega-Quiroga, I., Izquierdo, J., Medrano, M., Gysling, K., Pardo, L., Navarro, G., & Franco, R. (2021). Discovery of a macromolecular complex mediating the hunger suppressive actions of cocaine: Structural and functional properties. *Addiction Biology*, 26(5).

Bolivian authorities can push back the illicit market. Consequently, Bolivia's small farmers in the past were repeatedly caught in the crosshairs of the 'War on Drugs', with their fields being eradicated and growers ending up in prison. The Bolivians, however, see things a little differently. Why should they give up their centuries-old tradition just because people, mainly in the rich industrialized nations, can't keep their hands off cocaine? Why should this be a problem for the small Bolivian farmer who barely makes ends meet and chews coca from the barren garden to suppress hunger and thirst?

Bolivia acceded to the Single Convention in 1976. During the noughties, the country began to advocate for an amendment of the Single Convention and to remove the coca leaf from the list of prohibited narcotic substances. The attempt failed due to the resistance of several countries – including Germany. While Germany recognized that coca chewing was part of the cultural identity of the indigenous population of Bolivia, they had some fundamental doubts about changing the treaty regime. Instead, the German representatives proposed further dialogue on this with Bolivia and even a conference of states to discuss the issue. Other countries, such as the USA and Mexico, were less diplomatic. Most of them rejected Bolivia's proposal, arguing that they wanted to protect the integrity of the Single Convention.[16] Behind this was the deeply rooted concern that once you allow a change to the treaty regime, no matter how small, you open the door to further, more significant changes, ultimately leading to the abolishment of drug prohibition entirely.

After the amendment of the Single Convention was off the table, Bolivia's strategy was to obtain a subsequent reservation. Hence, in 2012, the Bolivian government initiated proceedings under Article 50(3) of the Single Convention. According to this article, a State Party may, under certain circumstances, subsequently obtain a reservation. While this procedure seems straightforward, it was not without risks. The rules stipulate that re-accession is only possible if not more than one-third of the signatory states (i.e., 61 out of 183) object within 12 months to the reservation. After the deadline had expired, only 15 state parties had objected to Bolivia's wish to re-enter the Convention. Among them were the USA, Canada – and Germany.[17]

Less than a decade later, Germany considered initiating the same procedure only his time for recreational cannabis. Bolivia has pioneered and demonstrated how the rigid treaty system can be disrupted and real change implemented. Germany did not only observe this historical endeavor from the sideline but actively opposed it. This means that Germany would have

16 Jelsma, M. (2011). Lifting the ban on coca chewing: Bolivia's proposal to amend the 1961 Single Convention. *Series on Legislative Reform of Drug Policies*, 11, 1–12.

17 See UNODC: Bolivia to re-accede to UN drug convention, while making exception on coca leaf chewing. https://www.unodc.org/unodc/en/frontpage/2013/January/bolivia-to-re-accede-to-un-drug-convention-while-making-exception-on-coca-leaf-chewing.html.

preferred to see Bolivia remain on the doorstep of the most important drug control treaty rather than accept a reservation. Bolivia was concerned with the chewing of coca, a centuries-old tradition practiced by some of the poorest people in the world to suppress hunger and thirst. Germany, one of the wealthiest countries in the world, desires to legalize cannabis for recreational use, i.e., for the pleasure of its citizens. The hypocrisy of such an endeavor is not without risk.

Will other signatory states remember Germany's double standards and, once Germany has left the treaties, object to a re-accession with reservation for cannabis? All it would take are 61 signatory states. Then it would be Germany being left outside of the most important drug control treaties. The consequences would be dire, not to mention the embarrassment for the self-declared international law-friendly state.[18]

Conclusion

The legal academic debate on cannabis legalization in compliance with international law has been going on for decades and has filled entire books. This chapter has only picked out a few aspects and outlined them briefly without claiming to give an exhaustive or complete picture of the situation. Other legal strategies, such as the inter se option or prioritizing the protection of human rights over drug prohibition, have been left out. A detailed analysis would go beyond the limited scope of this chapter, and these strategies have played only a minor role in the German debate. This, however, does not mean that these alternative legal strategies will play a role in the future.

The baseline is that while legalizing cannabis in signatory states for recreational purposes in compliance with international law is possible, it remains complicated, tedious, and bears numerous risks. Most signatory states that toy with the thought of cannabis legalization lack either this political conviction, patience, or willingness to risk ending up outside the treaty regime. Even more so, the fear is of a domino effect: If cannabis prohibition falls, other drugs will follow, and it is just a matter of time until the entire treaty system lies in shambles. There is little reason to believe that this would happen. But then again, that is the problem with fear: It is rarely based on reason.

Until October of 2022, the German government was determined to go through with full cannabis legalization in the form of a declaration or interpretation. In a so-called *Eckpunktepapier* (frameworkpaper), the German Ministry of Health states that it prefers the option of issuing a declaration of interpretation to the other parties to the international conventions and the

18 For a full discussion see Hofmann, R. (2023). The 'total-legalization' of cannabis in Germany: Legal challenges and the EU free market conundrum. *European Journal of Crime, Criminal Law and Criminal Justice*, 31(2), 173–196. https://doi.org/10.1163/15718174-bja10044.

international drug control bodies in which it declares the implementation of the coalition agreement (hence, the full legalization of cannabis)

> *to be compatible with the purpose and legal requirements of the conventions.*[19]

Interestingly enough, even the German government seemed to have some doubts as to how this unilateral declaration of interpretation could relativize Germany's obligations under international drug control treaties. It admits that the options for implementing the plans are limited and associated with various risks under international and European law. Curiously, the paper mentions the risk of being criticized by the International Narcotics Control Board or other signatories but not the procedure provided for in the treaty, namely, being taken to the International Court of Justice. However, another circumstance was clearly more decisive: The German government deemed it essential to ensure that the EU Commission and member states follow Germany's interpretation approach in order to minimize the risk of infringement proceedings and/or state liability claims, which would ultimately have to be decided by the Court of Justice of the European Union (CJEU). In order to avoid this, a close and transparent coordination with the EU Commission was announced. Indeed, soon after, a German governmental delegation visited the EU Commission in Brussels to inform about the plans. When the delegates returned to Germany, cannabis legalization was off the table, and so was the interpretation declaration. As to what was discussed in Brussels, we can only speculate as the content of the meeting has been kept secret until today. However, there is little doubt that the reasons for this historic turnaround are to be found in European law. However, there is no doubt that the reasons for this historic turnaround can be found in European law. In the following chapter, we will examine these reasons in detail.

19 German Government. (2022). *Eckpunktepapier der Bundesregierung zur Einführung einer kontrollierten Abgabe von Cannabis an Erwachsene zu Genusszwecken* (p. 2). German Government.

4 Cannabis and the EU

Introduction

So far, we have dealt with the tightly knitted prohibitive framework of international law when it comes to drugs in general and cannabis specifically. We have also seen how limited the instruments of the international legal regime are to enforce its own rules. However, this is of little relevance for Germany as adhering to the international rules is *Staatsräson* (reason of state), which has led to the development of more or less convincing legal strategies to make the envisaged legalization of cannabis possible. However, as it turned out, the European Union raised far bigger obstacles to the regulation plans through EU law. Opposed to international law, EU law is a tiger with many sharp teeth that is not afraid to bite. The EU Commission regularly uses so-called infringement procedures to sue member states before the Court of Justice of the European Union in Strasbourg whenever it alleges a violation of EU law.

The EU Commission has vast executive and legislative powers. It drafts political strategies for the Union and is a watchdog suspiciously scrutinizing the implementation of the treaties in the member states. However, there are also limitations to these powers of the European Union: In some areas, only the member states and not the EU itself have the power to create laws and regulations. The principle of subsidiarity enshrined in Article 5 of the Treaty of the European Union restricts the power of the EU wherever member states can achieve the goals of an intervention better by themselves.[1] In reality, however, the EU has gained increasing legislative powers over the years, having a say in many policy areas while leaving very few untouched. It is exactly within this area of tension between state sovereignty and the higher purpose of ensuring a unified approach where drug policies find themselves. This tension is exacerbated by the fact that EU law breathes a similar prohibitive spirit as the international drug control regime.

1 In there is also the exception of the exclusive competences of the EU which should not concern us here.

DOI: 10.4324/9781003503439-5

This chapter addresses the following questions: How does EU law relate to international law, and how does this impact drug prohibition? What laws and regulations does European law contain on cannabis, and how does this impact the member states' freedom to regulate the soft drug? More generally asked: Who is really in the driver's seat when it comes to drug policies? The international treaty regime? The European Union? Or the member states?

As a founding member of the European Union, Germany is bound by EU law just like the other 26 member states. This mainly consists of primary and secondary law. Primary law refers to the treaties concluded between the member states, i.e., the Treaty on European Union (TEU) and the Treaty on the Functioning of the European Union (TFEU). Secondary law is derived from the treaties such as regulations, directives, and recommendations. So-called framework decisions were also part of this secondary law and very similar to directives but were abolished by the Lisbon Treaty in 2009. However, for our context, this instrument in the form of a specific framework decision from 2004 will play a crucial role. Just like directives, framework decisions are defined by the fact that these are binding for the member states but only for the desired result to be achieved. While regulations are directly applicable in the member states, directives have to be transformed into domestic law first and, hence, provide the member states with some leeway as long as the overreaching goal of the directive is achieved. We will see later what this means for the context of cannabis and why this is important. Last but not least, the Court of Justice of the European Union case law plays a decisive role when assessing the impact of EU law on drug policies. In fact, the Court, in quite some instances, has dealt with drug and cannabis policies in the EU member states, with the most relevant decision being the Josemans Judgement from 2010. Curiously enough, the judgment originated in the city of Maastricht and a coffee shop called Easy Going, the same place where these very lines are written (meaning the city, not the coffee shop).

EU Health Policies and Drugs

There are two different perspectives from which one can look at drugs. The first perspective considers drugs first and foremost as a security risk. Trade, possession, and use are forbidden by law. Consequently, law enforcement will do whatever is necessary to prevent future breaches of the law and persecute and punish those who have breached the law, at least in theory. The reality is a bit different, but this should not concern us for now. The second perspective on drugs is a health perspective. Drugs constitute, first and foremost, a risk to human health. Drug addiction is a disease; those dependent on drugs must be treated as patients, while recreational drug consumers have to be protected from products below standards. Drug policies are about protection, not prohibition, and prevention of health risks, not punishment of crimes.

This fundamental dichotomy has already been discussed in Chapter 2. It was also made clear that, in reality, the two perspectives have many intersections, and the boundaries might often be more fluid than expected. However, with a view to EU policies and the principle of subsidiarity, the question of which perspective prevails achieves new relevance. In the discussion about cannabis, it is often brought forward that drug policies, and especially cannabis policy, are national policies. Each EU member state should be able to determine for itself how it protects the health of its citizens. This includes drugs, the licit ones such as nicotine and alcohol as well as the illicit ones. Indeed, EU member states already have different policies in place when it comes to protecting the health of their own citizens. The EU recognizes that the diversity of historically grown health policies should be preserved and that the competence to shape them autonomously should not be unnecessarily restricted.[2]

In Germany, for example, 16-year-olds are allowed to buy and drink beer. In Sweden, on the other hand, this would be unthinkable. There, alcohol is not only completely permitted from the age of 18 but almost the entire sale of alcoholic beverages is also in state hands. The German liberal approach to alcohol can be observed in the public drinking culture. Consuming alcohol in public parks and streets is nothing unusual; it is strictly forbidden in the Netherlands (as in most other European member states).

These differences are made possible as the EU health policy is guided by the premise that health policymaking is the sole national responsibility of the member states.[3] The EU may, however, complement the member states policies, encourage their cooperation, and support their activities whenever necessary. Hence, one could argue that since drug use and abuse are assigned to health policies, the EU has no say in how the member states deal with all related policy issues. The handling of medical cannabis differs already among EU member states, with a number of EU member states having approved cannabis as a medicine while others have not, e.g., France, Sweden, and Austria.[4] Furthermore, Article 168 of the TFEU supports the argument, which states that the Union shall *complement* the member states' action in reducing drug-related health damage, including information and prevention measures.

Hence, from a health policy point of view, there seems to be little against EU member states legalizing cannabis for recreational purposes.[5] However, this only applies under the premise of looking at drugs through the glasses of

2 See the EU website. https://www.bundesgesundheitsministerium.de/themen/internationale-gesundheitspolitik/europa/europaeische-gesundheitspolitik.html.

3 https://www.bundesgesundheitsministerium.de/en/international/european-health-policy.html.

4 (as of 2022).

5 See Deutscher Bundestag. (2023). *Unionsrechtlich eröffnete Regelungsfreiheiten der Mitgliedstaaten im Bereich Cannabis*. Ausarbeitung EU 6-3000-024/23, 37. https://www.bundestag.de/resource/blob/959066/2bbc73133791ba5b6ea5bd26a1af6e44/EU-6-024-23-pdf-data.pdf.

a health-related issue. This view could be too one-dimensional and does not sufficiently take into account the fact that drug policies reach deep into crime policies as well. To understand what this means, it is worth taking a look at the case law of the Court of Justice of the European Union (CJEU).

The Josemans Ruling of the Court of Justice of the European Union

In 2010, the CJEU in Strasbourg had to decide an unusual case.[6] A coffee shop operator from Maastricht named Josemans had filed a complaint against the mayor of the city. The case concerned the coffee shop Easy Going, located in close proximity to the river Maas and the busy center of the city filled with tourists and shoppers from the neighboring countries Germany and Belgium. Josemans was fighting the closure of his coffee shop by the municipality of Maastricht, represented by its mayor. What had happened? The mayor had decreed that access to coffee shops should only be allowed to people who were residents of the Netherlands. In this way, the municipality wanted to limit the rampant drug tourism in the city. On some weekends, it was estimated that up to 10,000 people from Germany, Belgium, and France came to Maastricht in order to visit one of the dozens of coffee shops in the city creating all sorts of nuisance for the inhabitants of the city.

However, Josemans continued to sell cannabis to tourists from abroad, violating this residency requirement in his coffee shop. When the municipality discovered this, the major declared the establishment temporarily closed. Josemans fought this decision in a Dutch court, and after two years, the case finally ended up in the Court of Justice of the European Union in Strasbourg. The plaintiff Josemans claimed that the residence requirement for coffee shop visitors would discriminate against EU citizens based on nationality, which is strictly prohibited in the EU (Art 18 TFEU). He claimed that cannabis is a product like any other, and as such, every EU citizen within the free market can purchase it.

In essence, Josemans' argument was that Dutch citizens were given preferential treatment over other EU citizens for no good reason. What if French wineries would sell their wine only to the French since other nationals could not appreciate the product's superiority? Or if German car manufacturers only sold their cars to Germans but not to the Italians as their reckless driving is well known? What if the Italians retaliated by stopping all sales of shoes and suits to Germany because their lack of fashion sense is a disgrace to their products? Clearly, these absurd scenarios would undermine the idea of a free market and violate the principles on which the EU is built. Why, then, should cannabis, a tolerated soft drug in the Netherlands, be treated any differently?

6 CJEU Judgment of 16 October 2010, Case C137/09 *Marc Michel Josemans v Burgermeester van Maastricht*.

The CJEU, however, did not follow Josemans' argumentation. It denied discrimination based on nationality because, technically, the prohibition to sell to tourists is based on residency in the Netherlands and not nationality. Theoretically, EU citizens can move to the Netherlands, achieve a residency permit, and visit coffee shops as much as they want. Moreover, cannabis, while maybe tolerated in the Netherlands, is a prohibited product in the EU market and, as such, not protected by the free market rules. The same applies, for example, to counterfeit handbags which may be sold on street markets. These are illegal products, and EU citizens do not have the right to sell or purchase them. More important than these intricate free market rules is a different issue that was addressed by the CJEU and has gone surprisingly unnoticed in the German legalization debate since then: The issue of drug tourism.

The Phenomenon of Drug Tourism in the EU

The problem of drug tourism was not new when the CJEU issued its Josemans decision. Since the mid-1990s, the issue has been discussed on the EU level.[7] Since then, it had been regularly put on the agenda by a member state that particularly suffered from the phenomenon: This member state was not the Netherlands but, curiously enough, Germany. For decades, Germany had struggled with the liberal cannabis policy of the neighboring Netherlands, voicing its fierce critique of the Dutch as being naïve while engaging in enhanced cross-border cooperation with law enforcement authorities to curb drug tourism.

In the Netherlands, with its liberal drug policy, the effects of this rather special form of tourism are felt, especially in big cities like Amsterdam. The mostly centrally located coffee shops have been a source of all kinds of public nuisance for years. This ranges from disturbances of the peace to increased traffic to all kinds of petty criminal activities in the vicinity of these establishments. Even though scientists repeatedly point out that very similar social dynamics occur around bars and pubs, the image of coffee shops and their clients has suffered considerably.[8] With the fading public support of what once was considered the pinnacle of Dutch liberalism and an integral part of the country's folklore, Dutch authorities tightened their reins in recent years and increasingly regulated coffee shops. Curbing the flourishing drug tourism is high on the political agenda but with very moderate success so far.

The effects of this failure are also felt on the other sides of the Dutch border, especially in Germany. The so-called ant-smuggling of cannabis and other

7 Council Resolution of 29 November 1996 on measures to combat the problem of drug tourism within the European Union (OJ C 375, p. 3).

8 Jacques, S., Rosenfeld, R., Wright, R., & Van Gemert, F. (2016). The effects of prohibition and decriminalization on drug market conflict: Comparing street dealers, coffeeshops, and cafés in Amsterdam. *Criminology & Public Policy*, 15(3), 843–875.

drugs, meaning small amounts brought over the border by people mostly for their personal consumption or for friends, poses quite a burden for law enforcement and courts, especially in the many border towns. Unlike the Dutch, the German police have no leeway in whether or not to prosecute minor crimes related to the smuggling of cannabis. Since police checks are more frequent at the national borders, people with drugs from the Netherlands are also caught more often. The public prosecutors' offices and courts are overburdened with the caseload despite trying to discontinue or dismiss as many cases as possible. No wonder, then, that the Dutch regulation to sell cannabis only to persons registered in the Netherlands was welcomed by Germany. However, the hope that this would also reduce border smuggling has not been fulfilled. Today, about 15 years later, the law has only been implemented sporadically. In Amsterdam, for example, the law was not implemented at all, as it was feared that this would only fuel the cannabis black market. Indeed, at places where the coffee shops complied with the residency rules quickly, black-market dealers took care of supplying rejected tourists with the desired drugs.

Admittedly, the impacts of Dutch cannabis tolerance in the country and bordering Germany are minor in view of the problems related to the professional illicit drug trade. But drug tourism can also have more serious impacts as, once again, became evident in Germany a few years ago. This time, not the Dutch were to blame, but the eastern neighbor, the Czech Republic. For years, a real crystal meth epidemic unfolded in parts of Bavaria and Eastern Germany, caused, among other things, by the lax attitude of Czech authorities towards illicit drug laboratories.[9] In the EU member state, the synthetic drug crystal meth is, of course, banned. But for some time, the enforcement of the ban has been lax, either because police capacities were lacking or because the problem was simply not taken seriously enough. The consequences of this policy were outsourced to Germany. Many consumers made their way over the open border to buy the widely available and cheap drugs. Drug-related crimes skyrocketed, and so did the health costs for addiction treatments in German facilities.

The latter is a good example of the dilemma that ultimately is related to the Schengen Area and the abolishment of border controls within the EU. The crystal meth epidemic, as much as the overburden of German courts with cannabis cases, may be related to drug policies in the neighboring countries. But both are caused by German citizens making their way over the border to acquire the drugs and bring them back home. Hence, the Dutch and the Czechs might take the standpoint that it is, first and foremost, a German problem mainly caused by its own failed drug prevention policies. The Germans, however, may take the view that member states, when forming the EU and abolishing border

9 Kistner, A. (2014). Germany's crystal meth pandemic. *DER SPIEGEL*. https://www.spiegel.de/international/germany/crystal-meth-becoming-more-popular-in-germany-a-958215.html.

controls, have agreed on a prohibitive approach to all drugs, including cannabis and, most certainly, crystal meth. Indeed, the Schengen Implementation Agreement has a number of very specific regulations when it comes to the prohibition of drugs. The Court of Justice of the European Union pointed to many of these problems related to drug tourism in the Josemans ruling. The court specifically points out that 'combating drug tourism and the accompanying public nuisance is part of combating drugs'.[10] In that sense, the EU forms a *Schicksalsgemeinschaft*, a community of destiny, where the drug policy of one member state almost always has an impact on other member states.

European Regulations on Cannabis

A coordinated drug policy is a priority within the EU. The question remains how such coordination can be best achieved. Which regulations apply to cannabis in the EU and how are these enforced? How do these regulations affect a member state's endeavor to legalize cannabis? Within the European legal framework there are, essentially, two regulations which are the most relevant when it comes to cannabis.

First, there is the so-called Convention implementing the Schengen Agreement (hereafter SIC). For many, 'Schengen' is synonymous with the abolition of border controls within the EU. Since this agreement consists of a whole series of different agreements, it is also referred to as the 'Schengen acquis'. While the original Schengen agreement was signed as early as 1985, it was the Schengen Implementation Convention of 1990 which contains concrete regulations for the implementation of a variety of rules and regulations. It was not put into force until five years later, in 1995, and only then were border controls stalled, at least for a handful of countries such as Germany, Spain, the Netherlands, and France. Other countries followed later. The agreements were amended and supplemented a few more times and finally enshrined as the Schengen acquis in the Treaty of Amsterdam in 1997 and integrated into EU law in 1999.

The SIC contains regulations not only on the European border regime but also a whole series of other regulations, for example, on cross-border law enforcement, on the exchange of data within the framework of the Schengen Information System, and on dealing with drug smuggling. One must bear in mind that the abolition of internal borders, or more precisely, border controls, was equivalent to a small revolution in Europe at the time. Some even feared that without border controls, the Schengen states would slowly cease to exist, dissolving in the Schengen area like organic material in a poisonous acid. These concerns explain why it took ten years from the first Schengen agreement (Schengen I) to the abolition of border controls in 1995. The Schengen

10 CJEU Judgment of 16 October 2010, Case C137/09 *Marc Michel Josemans v Burgermeester van Maastricht*, lit 65.

states played it safe. Today, we know that many of the concerns at the time were unfounded. The free movement of goods, persons, and workers acted like rocket fuel for the integration of Europe and its economic performance. However, transnational organized crime profited from this integration as well. Be it drug trafficking, human trafficking, or also the laundering of criminal funds – all these forms of crime cross and exploit national borders. While border controls have largely disappeared, the borders in law enforcement, judicial systems, and exchange of information, not to mention the political, cultural, and language barriers, kept existing. Of course, this does not mean that there was no cross-border crime in the era of European border controls. Nevertheless, we can see that the abolition of border controls, like globalization in general, has acted like a fire accelerator for transnational organized crime since the 1990s.

While this may not have been foreseeable in the mid-'80s, there was enough foresight to integrate a number of harmonization agreements to combat crime into the Schengen regime. Among them is Article 71 of the SIC, which deals with the fight against drug trafficking. In its first paragraph, it states that the contracting parties undertake all necessary measures to prevent and punish the illicit trafficking of narcotic drugs and psychotropic substances, including the direct or indirect sale of cannabis and the possession of such products and substances for sale or export. These measures are adopted in accordance with the existing United Nations Conventions. Paragraph 2 states the parties undertake to 'prevent and punish by administrative and penal measures the illegal export of narcotic drugs and psychotropic substances, including cannabis, as well as the sale, supply and handing over of such products and substances'.

Two aspects are particularly important here: Firstly, there are two explicit references to cannabis. This is remarkable because most conventions only speak of narcotic drugs in general terms and then specify in a table in the annex which substances are included. Here, however, it was important for the contracting parties to explicitly point out that also, and above all, the trade in cannabis remains prohibited. The second interesting aspect is the reference to the United Nations Conventions. This refers to the three conventions already analyzed in the last chapter. Some consider this reference a real door opener for cannabis regulation within the EU and argue that international conventions are higher-ranking laws. As soon as a Schengen signatory state has implemented a regulation in compliance with international law (e.g., through a reservation or a declaration of interpretation), the SIC rules must immediately stand back. It remains, however, highly doubtful that a simple reference in the SIC contains a mechanism that would relegate the EU to a seat in the auditorium when it comes to shaping drug policies.[11]

11 Hofmann, R. (2023). The 'total-legalization' of cannabis in Germany: Legal challenges and the EU free market conundrum. *European Journal of Crime, Criminal Law and Criminal Justice*, 31(2), 184. https://doi.org/10.1163/15718174-bja10044.

By now, the thrust of the European regulations should be clear: Schengen breathes the spirit of the international prohibition regime and even seems to want to surpass it. No word is to be found about exceptions to the prohibition of drugs for medical or scientific purposes. Nothing about more lenient approaches to drugs grown for personal use, as found in the 1988 UN Convention. The reasons for this may have to do with the fact that the founding fathers wanted to prevent more lenient approaches like those implemented by the Netherlands from spilling over across the then-no-longer-existing national borders. Either way, Schengen, from its very beginning, breathes the spirit of drug prohibition. The inclusion of cannabis demonstrates that the drug was not considered an issue of health policy and its regulation subject to state sovereignty but rather a security problem.

Is There a Backdoor in the SIC to Deviate From Prohibition?

In recent years, it was discussed among scholars if the SIC provides the contacting states with a backdoor to deviate from the strict prohibitive regime established by Schengen. The Final Act of the Convention contains a joint declaration which reads as follows:

> *In so far as a Contracting Party departs from the principle referred to in Article 71(2) in connection with its national policy on the prevention and treatment of addiction to narcotic drugs and psychotropic substances, all Contracting Parties shall adopt the necessary administrative measures and penal measures to prevent and punish the illicit import and export of such products and substances, particularly towards the territories of the other Contracting Parties.*

Again, the primary concern of a spillover effect on other Schengen states is mentioned if one state departs from the rules of the convention. More remarkable, however, is the fact that the convention apparently considers deviations from its rules under the condition that these policies target the prevention and treatment of addiction to narcotic drugs, which include cannabis. The question arises as to what exactly is meant by 'prevention and treatment of addiction'.

A clear answer to this question is not easy. If we look at the debates on legalization, the reasons given in favor are often health protection, youth protection, curbing the black market, and relieving police and the judiciary. However, the fact that addiction to cannabis can be effectively combated by regulating the drug is rarely mentioned. One could argue that through regulation and limits for potency the highly potent and hence, more addictive cannabis is pushed off the market by legal, less potent cannabis. However, the effect is likely to moderate at best, as this might be precisely where the highest black-market potential exists. Consumers who prefer exceptionally strong weed will simply keep on relying on the black market, and to prevent this dynamic, many legalization advocates are calling for no cap on potency at all. While it might make sense to maximize the curbing effect on the black market, this might be counterproductive when it comes to preventing addiction. Even when taking into account an alleged destigmatizing effect of cannabis regulation, resulting in more people with risky consumption patterns seeking professional help, the argument that cannabis regulation will have a preventive effect on addiction remains far-fetched. While there arguably might be health benefits, the prevention of addiction is very likely not one of them. Moreover, it is important to remember that while the strict cannabis prohibition is enshrined in Article 71, paragraphs 1 and 2, the exemption of the joint declaration only specifically refers to paragraph 2. It remains unclear what exactly this means, but based on a systematic interpretation, there are reasons to believe that contracting parties wanted to exclude the possibility of a party departing too far from the set-out rules by implementing a fully fledged legalization of cannabis.

The 2004 Framework Decision

Over the years, a whole series of regulations in the Schengen Implementing Convention have been deleted as they were either superfluous or already regulated elsewhere. Article 71, however, remained untouched and is still valid today. In 2001, however, something remarkable happened: The EU Commission began drafting a framework decision that specifically deals with drugs and drug trafficking. Framework decisions were legal instruments adopted in the so-called Third Pillar of the EU, which comprised police and judicial cooperation in criminal matters. Whenever the EU Commission wanted to strengthen and better coordinate (i.e., harmonize) an issue related to the fight against crime, it drafted a framework decision. Without going further into the technical details of the instrument that since has been abolished, what is important is the fact that framework decisions were binding with regards to the objective to be achieved but left the member states room for maneuvering about national implementation. EU member states had to transpose the regulations it contained into national law within a certain period of time.

After several years of drafting, in 2004 the EU Commission finally released Framework Decision 2004/757/JHA (hereafter just FD 2004) dealing with the threat and fight against illicit drug trafficking by putting a strong focus on a coordinated and harmonized law enforcement approach among member states. There are several reasons why the Commission felt the need to deal with drug trafficking at that time. International drug trafficking was taking off at the beginning of the noughties. With Europol, there was a European police office that specialized in transnational crime, which brought the problem increasingly into the focus of politics. Moreover, it had become clear that member state policies and enforcement strategies towards drugs had somewhat drifted apart.[12]

FD 2004 declares drug trafficking as a threat to the health, safety, and quality of life of EU citizens. This is followed by references to international conventions, definitions, and offenses, a definition of what exactly is meant by drug trafficking, and how law enforcement should respond to it. Article 2(1), for example, lists the long series of offenses that we already know from the Single Convention and which EU member states are obliged to criminalize. It states further:

> *Each Member State shall take the necessary measures to ensure that the following intentional conduct when committed without right is punishable: (a) the production, manufacture, extraction, preparation, offering, offering for sale, distribution, sale, delivery on any terms whatsoever, brokerage, dispatch, dispatch in transit, transport, importation or exportation of drugs.*

Then, under b., specific reference is made to 'cultivating the opium poppy, the coca bush or cannabis plant'. Within these few sentences, more precisely in the two words 'without right', some believe to have found the key to a full legalization of cannabis in compliance with EU law.[13] But before analyzing if this without right clause is the game changer an increasing number of scholars believe it to be, we'll have a quick look at a very obviously significant provision of the text. Almost hidden in paragraph 2 of Article 2 it states:

> *The conduct described in paragraph 1 shall not be included in the scope of this Framework Decision when it is committed by its perpetrators exclusively for their own personal consumption as defined by national law.*

This sentence enshrines the probably most progressive stance EU law has ever taken on the issue of drugs, while at the same time, it might easily be one of the most confusing provisions. In simple words, paragraph 2 acts like a track switch towards impunity. The conduct described in paragraph 1 (a and b) falls outside the scope of the Framework Decision, i.e., does not have to be criminalized by member states if the person acted exclusively for the purpose of its own personal consumption. Applied to cannabis, this means that whoever

12 Chatwin, C. (2003). Drug policy developments within the European Union: The destabilizing effects of Dutch and Swedish drug policies. *The British Journal of Criminology*, 43(3), 567–582; Tops, P., Van Spijk, L., Van Valkenhoef, J., & Van der Torre, E. J. (2018). *The Netherlands and synthetic drugs: An inconvenient truth*. Eleven International Publishing.

13 For an in depth review of the debate see Hofmann, 2023, 184 et.seqq.

produces or cultivates the drug solely for its own personal consumption can remain exempt from punishment under national law. Spanish courts were among the first to understand the implications of these regulations and the sentencing of people who had grown cannabis plants at home were halted.[14] The cannabis social clubs movement with its wide interpretation of the words 'personal use' gained momentum as well all over Europe.[15]

However, the wording of the Framework Decision is clear in that the member states can decide for themselves whether they want to continue to punish acts of personal consumption. Germany, contrary to Spain, after ratifying the Framework Decision, opted to leave their criminal laws unchanged and kept on punishing consumers if they grew their own cannabis. The reasons for that were manifold and were mainly of a political nature where a further liberalization of cannabis consumption was simply unwanted.

The Framework Decision leaves no doubt that cultivation outside of personal consumption, e.g., for sale on the black market, must remain punishable. It is important to keep that in the back of the head since the misunderstanding is widespread that a person who sells or gives cannabis to another person for personal consumption should also be exempt from punishment. While there is some validity to this argument, there is little doubt that the EU legislature did not want the dealer to be included in the impunity clause.

More confusing, however, is the fact that the 'personal use impunity clause' references all conducts enlisted in Article 2 a and b. But b. does not only include the cultivation of cannabis but also explicitly refers to the cultivation of coca bushes and opium poppy. A strict interpretation of Article 2 paragraph 2 would allow the EU member states to decriminalize the cultivation of cocaine and heroin as long as it is for the purpose of personal use only. While this would be unprecedented, and until today, no member state has enacted a law that allows the growing of opium poppies for personal consumption purposes, there is little doubt that this is an unintentional mistake leaving one wondering how much care went into drafting the Framework Decision.

The Without Right Clause as the Loophole to Legalize All Drugs

For almost two years, the German legislature was determined to fully legalize cannabis. It begs the question of how Germany contemplated achieving this while complying with EU law? The answer can be found in the two words

14 Marks, A. (2019). Defining 'personal consumption' in drug legislation and Spanish cannabis clubs. *International & Comparative Law Quarterly*, 68, 193–223.

15 Pardal, M., Decorte, T., Bone, M., Parés, Ò., & Johansson, J. (2020). Mapping cannabis social clubs in Europe. *European Journal of Criminology*, 19(5). https://doi.org/10.1177/1477370820941392.

'*without right*' included in Article 2 of the Framework Decision. According to this:

> *Each Member State shall take the necessary measures to ensure that the following intentional conduct when committed without right is punishable.*

This 'without right clause' is so decisive because it suggests the existence of a right to deviate from the strict duty to criminalize certain conducts related to drugs (enumerated in the following paragraphs of the Framework Decision). Unfortunately, the text does not specify which right it refers to. Even in the documents on the drafting process, there is no indication of what exactly the Council and the Parliament had in mind.[16] It begs the question: What could be such a right that allows cannabis to be cultivated, harvested, distributed, and sold in a member state?

The straightforward answer to this question would be that international conventions have already exempted the trade of drugs for medical and scientific purposes from strict prohibitions. Otherwise, cultivators, pharma companies, medical distributors, and even doctors prescribing the drugs would have to be criminalized for drug production and trade under international law. To avoid this, the international treaties speak of licenses that can be issued by treaty states to regulate the trade of drugs for medical purposes. This licensing system creates the right, and without such a right, any drug production or trade would be illegal. Hence, the reference in Article 2 of the Framework Decision.[17]

However, over the years among some legal scholars a different interpretation of the two short words 'without right' gained popularity. Among other things, their argument is based on the fact that while international law speaks of 'licenses' when it comes to drug production or trade for medical or scientific purposes, the Framework Decision deliberately uses the term 'right' instead of 'license'. This legal interpretation opens up a number of possibilities as it suggests that member states are not confined to medical or scientific licensing when creating a right to produce or trade drugs. Member states would be enabled to regulate cannabis within their national laws and those same laws would then function as rights required by the Framework Decision. In other words, the entire drug prohibition enshrined in the Framework Decision only applies if a member state has not taken matters into its own hands and created

16 Van Kempen, P., & Fedorova, M. (2014). *Internationaal recht en cannabis Een beoordeling op basis van VN-drugsverdragen en EU-drugsregelgeving van gemeentelijke en buitenlandse opvattingen pro regulering van cannabisteelt voor recreatief gebruik* (p. 136). Kluwer. The entire document is available here. https://repository.wodc.nl/handle/20.500.12832/2100.

17 Klip, A. (2014). *European criminal law: An integrative approach* (4th ed., 281). Intersentia; Van Kempen & Fedorova, 2014, 136.

a formal law legalizing cannabis, hence establishing a right to produce and trade the drug under national law.

Admittedly, this argumentation sounds rather circular as it would mean that EU law would oblige member states to criminalize drugs unless they legalize them by law. However, some arguments favor such an interpretation of the Framework Decision. Let's take a close look at them:

1. If the Framework Decision only wanted to exempt medical and scientific trafficking from criminalization, why does it not say so? In fact, medical or scientific purposes are not mentioned anywhere in the Framework Decision, nor in the SIC. But if medical or scientific purposes are not specifically mentioned as exceptions, it might be the case that the EU considered other exceptions to the strict prohibition as well.
2. The very choice of the word 'right' indicates that the EU wanted to go beyond medical and scientific purposes. If one looks at the international conventions, there is either talk of 'permission' or 'licenses' in connection with the exceptions for medical and scientific purposes. In fact, the initial wording included the term 'license' but was scrapped and replaced by the much broader term 'right'.[18]
3. The Framework Decision breathes the spirit of reform to break new ground in the encrusted drug prohibition regime. This is clearly demonstrated by Article 2 paragraph 2 where personal consumption is privileged. These new paths may very well include giving the member states new and further leeway in their efforts to pursue alternative drug policies.

However, there are some arguments that speak against such a broad interpretation of the Framework Decision.

1. There is little evidence indicating that the words 'without right' would refer to something other than the exceptions of medical and scientific purposes. After all, in the entirety of international law, no other exception exists. Why and how would EU law establish other exceptions, especially as it references explicitly international law in Article 1, establishing that it accepts this as a guiding star?
2. One should not look so closely at the wording of the Framework Decision. The fact that 'without right' is broader than the terms 'permission' or 'license' says little. EU documents are translated into all EU languages, and the fine nuances can sometimes get lost in translation. Article 2 of the Framework Decision shows that the EU legislature is not very precise in its wording: It literally states that the member states may allow personal cultivation of the cannabis plant, the opium poppy, and the coca bush.

18 Van Kempen & Fedorova, 2014, 136.

There is little doubt that this is a mistake, and hence, the literal interpretation of the Framework Decision needs to be done with caution.

3. The Framework Decision only at its surface and only in Article 2 paragraph 2 breathes the spirit of a more liberal drug policy. The mere fact that the EU found it necessary to reaffirm the obligations of the member states to sanction drug trafficking only a little more than ten years after the SIC shows how serious the EU is about a uniform and, above all, restrictive drug policy. In this respect, the Framework Decision is independent, contains its own regulations, and is not just an appendix to international law. This also results from the reference to the international conventions that only apply in Article 1 and only to definitions. In the preamble, on the other hand, only European agreements are cited, which is intended to make clear: The EU follows its own drug policy with its own rules that apply equally in all member states. This includes the strict prohibition of cannabis.
4. The EU's legislative instruments always aim to harmonize the laws of the member states. It would be absurd for the EU to issue a framework decision that leaves the member states free to shape their drug policies by either prohibiting or legalizing all drugs. That simply cannot have been what the EU had in mind.

Other arguments in the debate seem to support neither of the interpretations. For example, the Court of Justice of the European Union in the aforementioned Josemans decision, although specifically dealing with Article 2 of the Framework Decision, mentions with no word that it opens up the possibility for member states to legalize cannabis through their own law. As the Court dealt with specific issues related to the Dutch tolerance approach to cannabis, one would think the judges would have mentioned the possibility if it had existed. But then again, the decision did not directly deal with legalization, so a reference by the Court was not required. An orbiter dictum, i.e., a clarification of the range of the without right clause by the Court, would have potentially put an end to the debate once and for all.

Conclusion

The legal debate about the without right clause is fascinating in many respects. It demonstrates how complex the regulation of cannabis is under EU law but also to what great length legalization advocates are willing to go and how much creativity goes into identifying some wiggle room in an otherwise encrusted prohibitive system. Often these suggested solutions and interpretations are mildly convincing at best. However, in the spirit of full disclosure, the conservative and rather skeptical stance taken by the author prioritizing a rather strict legal interpretation of the regulation is not the dominant point of view within the cannabis debate. In fact, it even seems that the interpretation of the 20-year-old Framework Decision has even changed in recent years towards a more lenient stance – despite the fact there were no changes in the EU legal framework or within the relevant CJEU jurisprudence. An interesting example of this is two of the most distinguished scholars in the field, Van Kempen and Federova, authors of a comprehensive legal assessment of legalizing recreational cannabis in the Netherlands from 2014. Back then, the authors concluded: 'We have found no evidence that the term "without right" in Article 2(1) is intended to have a broader scope'.[19] Moreover, the authors write: 'The final conclusion is that legalization, decriminalization, policy-based tolerance and/or other forms of regulating cannabis cultivation for the recreational user market is not permissible under the UN Narcotic Drugs Conventions or European law'.[20] About a decade later, the very same authors write

> *Authorization under the licensing system can as such very well qualify as a 'right' for the cultivator, distributor or salesperson to perform the activity. Authorization would thus mean that the activity does not take place 'without right' in the sense of Article 2(1) of the Framework Decision.*[21]

Even more, they argue that since cannabis regulation ensures more effective protection of human rights, it provides for a 'right' justifying deviation from obligations to criminalize cannabis for recreational use under the Framework Decision.[22]

While it might be normal for different legal scholars to have different opinions on controversial topics, it is less common for the same legal scholars to develop different opinions within a period of several years. But while we can only speculate about what caused this change of heart, it demonstrates how controversial the regulation of cannabis in compliance with EU law really is. It was this legal framework that ultimately let Germany backtrack from its far-reaching plans of a 'total' legalization of cannabis. At the end of the day, implementing what must be called probably the most significant change in drug policies of the past half-century on the basis of the interpretation of two words in the 20-year-old Framework Decision seems to be a risky endeavor.

19 The Dutch original formulation is: 'Wij hebben geen aanwijzingen kunnen vinden dat de term "rechtvaardigingsgrond" in artikel 2 lid 1 aanhef Kaderbesluit een ruimere strekking beoogt te hebben'. Van Kempen & Fedorova, 2014, 136.

20 Van Kempen & Fedorova, 2014, 4.

21 Van Kempen, P., & Fedorova, M. (2023). Cannabis regulation through the 'without right' clause in article 2(1) of EU framework decision 2004/757/JHA on illicit drug trafficking. *European Journal of Crime, Criminal Law and Criminal Justice* (published online ahead of print), 17. https://doi.org/10.1163/15718174-bja10039.

22 Van Kempen & Fedorova, 2023.

5 Cannabis Regulation Around the World

Introduction

We have seen that the regulation of cannabis does not take place in national isolation protected by state sovereignty or the current political zeitgeist. Rather, it is integrated into a widely branched regime of treaties and regulations, some more, some less reasonable. In criminal law, there is the unwritten principle that a law is only as good as its enforceability. In other words: The best contract is pointless if there are no mechanisms to enforce the rules in case of doubt. We have seen that these enforcement mechanisms exist in a weaker form in international law and in a stronger form in European law. Despite these strict rules and enforcement instruments, a number of countries have left the canon of prohibition in recent years and implemented alternative policy models for cannabis. But what policy models exist, and how are these conceptualized? How have other countries overcome the legal obstacles posed by international and European law? What are the advantages and disadvantages of these alternative models? How have these affected the neuralgic issues of cannabis regulation, the prevalence of the drug, the protection of minors, and the black market? What can we learn from the mistakes of other countries? Can successful models be transferred to other countries with the same expected outcome? Can what works well in Canada, for example, also work in Germany? Are black-market developments occurring in Ontario similar to developments in Osnabrück after legalization? Is the consumer behavior of young people in Bern comparable to that of young people in Berlin?

Of course, one should be cautious when making comparisons with such countries. A myriad of factors may play a role, including societal, political, and legal ones. Nevertheless, to simply ignore experiences from other countries would be downright negligent and, moreover, not very scientific. Without giving too much from the last chapter of this book when the German cannabis law is discussed in detail: The German approach to full legalization of cannabis was astonishingly ignorant of other countries' experiences with regulation. In fact, the German health minister explicitly stated when

DOI: 10.4324/9781003503439-6

asked about his strategy that the Netherlands is not a role model.[1] While knowing what one does not want might be a first step, it is no substitute for a prudent, realistic, and above all feasible regulatory strategy. In Germany, however, this was precisely what was lacking, and all attempts to make up for this omission at a later date ended in a watering down of the original plans until there was not much left of them. But more about that in the concluding chapter.

The UN Drug Report 2022 states that cannabis is cultivated in almost all countries of the world. In the vast majority of countries, however, cannabis remains illegal. In 64 countries, cannabis is permitted for medical purposes, although the individual systems vary considerably.[2] The countries in which cannabis is generally illegal should not interest us here. More interesting, however, are the countries that have tried in recent years and decades to implement alternative routes within the narrow margins set by the international drug control treaties, sometimes to overstretch them or even to leave them behind altogether. All these alternative models are characterized by the will to break new ground and leave behind drug prohibition, which is perceived as arbitrary, patronizing, and all too often counterproductive.

This chapter will look at the cannabis policies of a few selected countries. This selection is subjective, the analyses no more than spotlights. The aim is merely to show by way of example which alternative paths are open in cannabis policy, if and how these are in compliance with the law, and what can be learned from there for regulating cannabis.

The Dutch Approach: (Not) A Role Model for Germany?

It has already been mentioned that the German government modeled its regulatory approach on the Netherlands as a negative example and focused on avoiding the alleged mistakes the Dutch neighbors had made over the years. That is reason enough to have a closer look at the unique Dutch leniency towards soft drugs with its world-famous coffee shops that not only have become tourism magnets but, over time, become deeply engraved in the country's folklore. But while the Dutch tolerance towards cannabis has been praised by proponents of legalization, considerable cracks have appeared in the façade of the nation's model in recent years. How does the Dutch regulatory model work? What problems occurred over the years, and how do the Dutch try to solve them?

1 See here https://www1.wdr.de/nachrichten/cannabis-freigabe-lauterbach-legalisierung-100.html.

2 UNODC. (2022). *World drug report 2022, drug market trends cannabis opiods*. UNODC. https://www.unodc.org/res/wdr2022/MS/WDR22_Booklet_3.pdf.

Today, there are over 500 so-called coffee shops in the Netherlands. In addition to coffee and non-alcoholic beverages, these local shops offer cannabis in different variations for sale to adult customers. They can take home up to 5 grams of the soft drugs for their own use or consume them right away in the store. The latter is also the reason why a coffee shop can usually be recognized from afar by the sweet smell of weed wafting through the neighboring alleys. The shops often have names that are programmatic like Easy Going, Slow Motion, or Relax; sound seductive like Extase or Heaven 69; or seem openly conspiratorial like Grey Area or Risky Business. These conspiratorial titles, in particular, describe the Dutch policy better than the people who gave them their names probably had in mind. While the coffee shops may be famous, what is less well known is that these operate in the legal grey area. Some might even consider the term grey as a euphemism for what is, in essence, an illegal operation.

It may come as a surprise to some readers that cannabis is not legal in the Netherlands. In fact, Article 3 of the Dutch Narcotics Law (Opiumwet) clearly prohibits the substances listed in List II, which also includes cannabis. This is followed by an enumeration of all kinds of offenses, such as bringing, cultivating, preparing, treating, processing, selling, delivering, making available, transporting, etc., the substance within or outside the territory of the Netherlands. List II of the law contains the so-called soft drugs, while List I describes hard drugs. The former include cannabis and certain psychedelic mushrooms, while hard drugs include heroin, cocaine, and synthetic drugs such as XTC.

This distinction between soft and hard drugs can be called the backbone of the Dutch drug policy. It is based solely on the assessment of health risks, such as the physical and psychological risks of addiction. The classification allows the Dutch legislature to introduce specific and adapted regulations for soft drugs and by not classifying cannabis in the same category as cocaine or heroin, different regulations can be set for it. It is a simple but effective trick that has given Dutch politicians, and especially law enforcement officers considerable leeway. This distinction has ultimately remained unique to the Netherlands and was never accepted internationally. This concept has not been adopted in any of the drug control treaties, and I am not aware of any other countries that have implemented this classification in their laws. The reason for this might be that there remain some problems with this distinction. Most importantly the distinction itself is somewhat arbitrary. For example, there are those who claim that the health risk potential of tobacco is at least as high as that of THC. Tobacco, however, is not included in the list of soft drugs. On the other hand, drugs like MDMA and LSD do not really fit into the hard drug scheme, as the addictive consequences are relatively low compared to alcohol, for example. Moreover, the health risks of cannabis have increased enormously as the plants have become more potent over the years. As already mentioned, the intoxicating effect of some of today's weed has little in common with the harmless hippie drug of the 1970s.[3] Especially with this increasingly popular high-potency cannabis, the Dutch are increasingly getting into a quandary: According to the strict criteria of health risk, high-potency cannabis should no longer qualify as a soft drug. Therefore, the Dutch legislature has introduced a kind of threshold value: As soon as the active substance content of 15% THC is exceeded, the cannabis is reclassified as a hard drug. Why exactly at 15% and not at 10% or 20%? The legislature does not have a clear answer to this question.

In the Netherlands, at least, this classification has existed for years, and it forms the basis for what is called the tolerance policy towards soft drugs. But how does this tolerance work when criminal law clearly states that *all* drugs, including soft drugs, are prohibited? This has to do with another peculiarity of the Dutch criminal justice system, the so-called opportunity principle. If the distinction between soft and hard drugs is the backbone of the Dutch system, the opportunity principle could be called the skull bone: It contains the brain of the Dutch approach to drugs and crime in general. It is worth going back a little further in history to understand why this approach is so crucial and, moreover, the exact opposite of the German approach to drugs.

The Historical Origin of Dutch Coffee Shops

Tolerance towards cannabis originated in the 1970s, in the summer of 1972 to be precise. It was not cannabis that started this development but, curiously enough, the much more dangerous heroin. That summer, cheap heroin appeared on the streets of Amsterdam for the first time. Within a very short time, the drug spread to all the big cities in the country with all its negative consequences. At about the same time, cannabis had established itself as a drug of the academic middle class, as an expression of a young and liberal counterculture that was celebrated on university campuses. There was no sign that cannabis would become popular beyond this narrowly defined youth culture, and the problems associated with it appeared manageable to law enforcement agencies. Concerning, however, was the fact that the same dealers who put heroin on the market also had cannabis on offer, hence endangering the cannabis users from getting in contact with the hard drug.[4]

The police and prosecution services, having their hands full trying to control the heroin market, were looking for a pragmatic solution. They found it in a separation of the drug markets by officially turning a blind eye to cannabis.

3 Caulkins, J. P., Kilmer, B., & Kleiman, M. A. R. (2016). *Marijuana legalization: What everyone needs to know* (2nd ed., pp. 12–13). Oxford University Press.

4 Van de Bunt, H., & Muller, T. (2021). The bankruptcy of the Dutch cannabis policy: Time for a restart. In H. Nelen & D. Siegel (Eds.), *Contemporary organized crime, studies of organized crime* (Vol. 18, p. 14). Springer.

In 1976, the Dutch public prosecutor's office decided it would tolerate the consumption and possession of cannabis. With this tolerance, the black market changed abruptly but in a different way than initially expected. This approach was based on the assumption that the few consumers would grow some plants at home and consume the weed themselves or with friends. Small amounts would be available in the protected spaces of coffee houses, with the profit motive clearly in the background. Today, we can see how wrong they were. In a short time, the cannabis business developed into a booming business, and coffee shops popped up everywhere, first in the big cities, then increasingly in the border areas. Abroad, word of the tolerance policy spread quickly, and within years the coffee shops became the tourist magnets they are today.

It was soon realized that not only the business's scale was underestimated, but a crucial regulatory loophole had also been left open: While the coffee shops were allowed to sell small quantities for private use, it remained unclear where they were supposed to get the large quantities of cannabis to supply their costumers? After all, the tolerance of law enforcement had never been intended to exempt organized criminals, the large cannabis growers and dealers importing the drug from abroad from punishment. The Dutch call this the 'backdoor problem': Cannabis goes out the front door legally but comes in the backdoor illegally.[5] Later and in order to create some legal security for the coffee-shop operators, a maximum of 500 grams was allowed to be in storage in order to be sold. This, however, did not solve the issue of the illegal sources for this cannabis. One might call it the birth defect of Dutch cannabis policy with dire consequences that are haunting the country's drug and crime policies until this very day.

The Dutch Opportunity Principle

To understand what went wrong and why this initial mistake was not corrected later, one needs to familiarize oneself with a peculiar trait of the Dutch legal system: The opportunity principle. This principle gives the Dutch investigating authorities discretion in deciding which offenses to prosecute and which not. A number of aspects may play a role in this decision, such as criminal policy priorities, capacity reasons, prospects of success of the investigation, efficiency aspects, or the seriousness of the offenses to be prosecuted. In round tables (so-called weegploegen), city mayors, police, and public prosecutors define the focal points of criminal prosecution to determine which crimes are prioritized and which are not.[6] This procedure is very much the opposite of

5 Buruma, Y. (2007). Dutch tolerance: On drugs, prostitution, and euthanasia. *Crime & Justice*, 73–113.

6 Hofmann, R. (2022). Formalism versus pragmatism – a comparative legal and empirical analysis of the German and Dutch criminal justice systems with regard to effectiveness and efficiency. *Maastricht Journal of European and Comparative Law*, 28(4), 452–478.

the legality principle we encountered in Chapter 2, which is the leading principle for enforcing the law in Germany: Every criminal offense that comes to the attention of law enforcement authorities must be investigated and prosecuted. While, overall, the two neighboring legal systems are very similar and built on the same legal traditions, this difference in the principles governing law enforcement is remarkable in many ways. Two different legal cultures are evident here, one with a tendency towards formalism and a doctrinal way of thinking, the other with a more pragmatic approach. This was aptly captured by the two legal scholars Blankenburg and Bruinsma in their book on Dutch legal culture:

> *The Dutch tend to be pragmatic. They use law to solve problems not to create additional ones. If applying the rules would lead to serious disadvantages, the Dutch try to find ways around them. Rules too strict to be applied are ignored and if that meets with resistance, they change them.*[7]

The tolerance policy towards cannabis is a good example of this Dutch pragmatism. But it also produced some rather unique consequences, which may be the reason that the approach remained unique and was never copied by other countries. The dynamics and consequences of this approach can best be illustrated by the so-called Checkpoint case and is described by Van den Bunt and Muller in their text on 'The Bankruptcy of the Dutch Cannabis Policy'.[8] Checkpoint was one of the largest coffee shops in the country, located in the city of Terneuzen near the border with Belgium. In the 1990s, the city allowed the coffee shop to open in order to curb the growing black market in drugs. However, the coffee shop was more of a 'coffee shopping center' with its own restaurant and over 100 employees. At its best in the mid-noughties, the coffee shop had 2500 to 3000 customers and sold between 10 and 15 kilos of cannabis a day.[9] The city granted a special car park and Terneuzen's mayor invited colleagues from other cities for tours, where he presented Checkpoint as the ideal modern coffee shop. But how was all this possible when the amount of cannabis a coffee shop was allowed to stock was limited to half a kilo?

The public prosecutor's office probably also asked itself this question before it had Checkpoint searched in 2007. The mayor had not been informed. There were concerns about the mayor's friendly attitude towards the owners and that information about the search could be leaked in advance. The prosecution seized 96 kilos of cannabis, 4.5 kilos of which were seized from the coffee shop itself. Checkpoint was temporarily closed and the owner taken

7 Blankenburg, E., & Bruinsma, F. (1994). *Dutch legal culture* (2nd ed.). Deventer.
8 Van de Bunt & Muller, 2021, 11–23.
9 Van de Bunt & Muller, 2021, 20.

into custody. Soon, however, the coffee shop was open again at the instigation of the mayor, who saw a danger to public order if sales could not be resumed soon. Then, a year later, there was another search. This time 4 kilos of cannabis were seized. This was followed by the permanent closure of Checkpoint and years of litigation in which the owner and staff of the coffee shop had to answer for forming a criminal organization. In the end, some of the defendants were sentenced to short prison terms, whereby the court also took into account that both the city, public prosecutor's office, and tax authorities had known about the magnitude of the sales for years and that the owner had never made a secret of it. The sentences were partially overturned by the Dutch Supreme Court a few years later.

Contradictions of the Dutch Tolerance Policy

The Checkpoint case is a good example of the contradictions in Dutch cannabis policy. Contradictions have become more and more apparent in recent years. In fact, there is not much left of the Dutch tolerance policy, which – it must be said – was characterized by a good portion of ignorance and naïvety from the beginning. All attempts to recapture the spirit that had been let out of the bottle had cosmetic effects at best. Coffee shops are integrated into a strict system of regulations and requirements: In addition to a general ban on advertising, a ban on alcohol, and a minimum distance from schools, the coffee shop operators are also obliged to take active action against nuisance and disturbances of public safety around their establishments. The debate about nuisance created by drug tourism, street dealers in the vicinity of coffee shops, and the reliance on organized crime in order to operate has been going on for years without much progress.[10] Hence, the acceptance of coffee shops among the population has suffered. This has led to the number of coffee shops falling from 1460 in the mid-1990s to around 550 today. The majority of Dutch municipalities now oppose the opening of new coffee shops.[11] At the same time, the regulatory corset is being tightened. Amsterdam, for example, banned the public consumption of cannabis in the city center in 2023 in order to make the city more livable for its residents. Even after more than four decades, the Dutch coffee shops are still far from being normal businesses.

The fact that Dutch tolerance has suffered in recent years cannot be blamed on cannabis and coffee shops alone. In fact, these developments have to be seen in the broader context of the global drug trade and the role that the

10 See for example Jacques, S., Rosenfeld, R., Wright, R., & Van Gemert, F. (2016). The effects of prohibition and decriminalization on drug market conflict: Comparing street dealers, coffeeshops, and cafés in Amsterdam. *Criminology & Public Policy*, 15(3).

11 Van de Bunt & Muller, 2021, 22.

Netherlands plays in it. The country today is the central gateway for drugs into the European market. The port of Rotterdam is one of the most important transshipment points for cocaine worldwide. The southern provinces of Limburg and Brabant are something like the Silicon Valley of synthetic drugs: A Dutch ecstasy pill costs a few cents to produce. On the Australian market it fetches 25 dollars.[12] Dutch cannabis, also called 'nederwiet' is of top quality and is grown in remote barns and attics all over the country. Eighty percent of the product is destined for export. The Province Noord Brabant holds the title of 'weed barn' of Europe. Turnover here alone is estimated at around 1 billion euros a year, and around 2500 people work in the illegal cannabis business there.[13] The negative effects of the drug business on society and the environment are fatal. Conflicts between drug gangs are increasingly fought out on open streets. Executions occur frequently, and far too often, uninvolved people are caught in the line of fire. Chemical waste from the production of synthetic drugs is illegally dumped in nature, with hundreds of such dumps identified by the police every year. Journalists, politicians, and justice officials are increasingly caught in the crosshairs of criminal gangs.

What does all this have to do with cannabis and the coffee shops? For one thing, a historical connection can be made between the emergence of the first coffee shops in the 1970s and the country's central position in the European drug trade today. Over time, criminal networks formed to smuggle cannabis from Morocco and Turkey into the Netherlands to meet the demand of coffee shops. Over the years, these networks professionalized and refined the operational business and the distribution channels. Then, in the late '80s, with the rise of cocaine, and in the '90s, with the explosion of demand for synthetic drugs, the organized criminals diversified their business and used the established channels for more lucrative drugs than cannabis.

But Dutch tolerance has had an even more subtle effect on drug trafficking. Besides the advantageous geographical location in the heart of Europe, the mild penal climate is also the ideal breeding ground for organized drug crime. Comparatively lenient sentences for drug dealers, remarkably comfortable prisons, and restrained prosecution over many years are symptoms of the same tolerance and have contributed to the rise of the Netherlands as an attractive location for drug traffickers. Pieter Tops, a well-known Dutch criminologist, considers it an inconvenient truth that '[d]rug producers benefit from this laidback stance. For a long time, they have met with little resistance, except when other countries put pressure on the Netherlands'.[14]

12 Tops, P., Van Spijk, L., Van Valkenhoef, J., & Van der Torre, E. J. (2018). *The Netherlands and synthetic drugs: An inconvenient truth* (p. 67). Eleven International Publishing.

13 Van de Bunt & Muller, 2021, 18.

14 Tops et al., 2018, 36.

The Future of Cannabis in the Netherlands: The Wietexperiment?

How will the Netherlands deal with the problems that arise in connection with the backdoor problem and organized crime in the near future? The Dutch have toyed with the idea of full legalization in order to replace the tolerance policy with robust and full cannabis legalization. Unlike in Germany, however, before embarking on such a complex and far-reaching endeavor, Dutch legal scholars carefully examined the legal possibilities and came to the conclusion that full cannabis legalization would not be compatible with either international nor European law.[15] Previously, the Court of Justice of the European Union had basically decided that the Dutch tolerance policy, including the coffee shop system, may be just in compliance with EU law.[16] Beyond that, however, there is no room for legal maneuvers. Then, in 2017, some movement appeared in the deadlocked Dutch situation: After weighing all options, the government decided to carry out the so-called Wietexperiment. The idea is extensive pilot studies with ten Dutch municipalities in which coffee shops are supplied with cannabis from legal cultivation.[17] The aim of the model experiment is to clarify whether the entire value chain, from cultivation to supply to sale in the coffee shops, can be handled in a state-controlled manner. This would render the backdoor problem a thing of the past and give coffee shops a secure and sustainable foundation. The entire experiment is closely and regularly assessed by a scientific commission gathering empirical data on the impact of cannabis consumption and developments on the black market.

However, from its beginning the experiment ran into considerable problems and challenges. Initially, the plan was to finish the experiment by 2024. With numerous delays and postponements, the experiment started its first trial phase in two municipalities by the beginning of 2024. In September 2024, the experiment should officially start in all municipalities.[18] It is obligatory for all coffee shops in the ten test communities to take part in the experiment as they otherwise risk losing their licenses. This compulsory participation is a crucial prerequisite for the experiment in order to shield the participating coffee shops from their illegally supplied counterparts by offering cheaper or more potent

15 Van Kempen, P. H., & Federova, M. (2014). *Internationaal recht en cannabis: Een beoordeling op basis van VN-drugsverdragen en EU-drugsregelgeving van gemeentelijke en buitenlandse opvattingen pro regulering van cannabisteelt voor recreatief gebruik*. Kluwer.

16 CJEU Judgment of 16 October 2010, Case C137/09, *Marc Michel Josemans v Burgermeester van Maastricht*.

17 See https://www.rijksoverheid.nl/onderwerpen/experiment-gesloten-coffeeshopketen-wietexperiment.

18 See the information by the government. https://www.rijksoverheid.nl/onderwerpen/experiment-gesloten-coffeeshopketen-wietexperiment/nieuws/2024/03/15/overgangsfase-van-experiment-gesloten-coffeeshopketen-wietexperiment-start-in-juni.

cannabis. However, having little to say in the process resulted in rather moderate enthusiasm among coffee shop operators.

A call for tenders followed for companies to grow the cannabis for the model trial. The interest was huge, with over a hundred start-ups wanting to be at the forefront and the process being broadcast on national TV. However, only a few companies remained after being fiercely scrutinized by authorities in compliance with the so-called BIPOP Act, laws aimed at preventing organized criminals from participating in tenders and thus infiltrating the legal economic cycle. In the end, seven applicants remained who were to take over the cannabis production and supply the coffee shops with state-licensed weed. Many of the entrepreneurs encountered resistance to opening company bank accounts due to perceived money laundering risks. Moreover, many of the mostly rural communities in which the weed greenhouses were to be built were not very enthusiastic about the cannabis farmers. They feared that organized criminals could infiltrate the young enterprises or sabotage the cultivation by force. The greenhouses resemble high-security penitentiaries: The cannabis and all processes must, of course, be strictly secured and monitored, as a top priority is to prevent cannabis from ending up on the black market. Thus, delivery to the coffee shops is also done in armored vehicles, which are usually used for bank transports. Another issue that occurred during the implementation phase of the experiment, leaving state officials increasingly concerned, was that tobacco companies had begun to invest money into the newly established cannabis growers.

Despite these more practical problems, the question remains how well the experiment is legally founded. After all, the Dutch state is not only tolerating but actively facilitating the large-scale production and supply of an illicit substance for non-medical purposes. However, due to the design as an experiment that includes rigorous scientific evaluation, the legal rationale clearly speculates on the treaty exemption for scientific reasons. Whether this is sufficient to be in line with the provisions of the drug control treaties and EU law remains to be seen. Rumor has it that the European Commission has sent a letter to the Dutch government in order to inquire about the experiment, usually the initial step before initiating an infringement procedure. Maybe more important is a different issue: Experiments, by definition, have an expiry date. The gathered data are analyzed and compounded in a final report. Conclusions are drawn, and recommendations are formulated. But what happens after the experiment is wrapped up and assessed positively? Will it be extended, maybe indefinitely? Or is it built on the hope that by then, drug laws and treaty obligations with a view to cannabis have changed? Or do the Dutch speculate the experiment will supply the arguments and empirical data to change international EU law? Either way, there seems to be no strategy in place or at least no published information on how to proceed after the experiment is finalized.

Cannabis in Switzerland: Legalization Despite Bad Experiences

After the Netherlands in Europe, it is Switzerland which has taken a rather unconventional approach to cannabis. There, too, a number of pilot studies are currently implemented, made possible by a change in the law that came into force in May 2021. According to the Swiss Federal Office of Public Health (FOPH), the trials are limited to a period of ten years, are scientifically monitored, and are intended to provide a scientific basis for a full regulation of cannabis in the future. For everyone interested in cannabis regulation, it is worth taking a look at the FOPH's website. There is an impressive archive of articles, papers, studies, analyses, and further literature in several languages on cannabis in general and the Swiss regulatory plans specifically. In addition to comprehensive legal documents and questionnaires for the empirical monitoring of the pilot trials, there are also extensive evaluations of the data available to date from other countries. It shows, for example, that the Swiss experts have studied the Canadian legalization model in depth, especially the so-called Good Production Practices for cannabis.[19] A study by the University of Bern assessed the contamination of black-market cannabis by pesticides in Switzerland.[20] It showed that most cannabis products from police seizures are contaminated with pesticides or with microbiological contamination, for example, in the form of fungi/spores and bacteria. Particularly interesting is a paper on the protection of minors in regulated cannabis markets.[21] As a reminder, this is one of the sore points when it comes to regulatory models. How can young people be protected from contaminated or highly potent cannabis, as well as the dangers of the black market, if cannabis is only legally available to adults? The paper points out an often overlooked risk coming with the approval for adult use: It may have the adverse effect that young people may become the focus of attention of law enforcement. Freed-up police capacities are likely to be focused on the black market, which is mostly frequented by minors. Proposed solutions to this problem, however, remain only partly convincing. For example, the authors toy with the idea of allowing the purchase of cannabis from the age of 16, but under the condition that young people take part in a cannabis discussion group twice a year. This scenario seems rather unrealistic.

19 Lardos, A. (2021). *Vergleich zwischen den Good Agricultural and Collection Practices (GACP) der Europäischen Arzneimittel-Agentur (EMA) und den kanadischen Good Production Practices für Cannabis*. Zürcher Hochschule für angewandte Wissenschaften.

20 Bernhard, W., Ambach, L., König, S., Nussbaumer, S., & Weinmann, W. (2017). *Testing of cannabis for extenders, blends, pesticides, microbiological and inorganic contaminants*. Universität Bern.

21 Baumberger, P., Bücheli, A., Grob, A., Hubrich, R., Rindlisbacher, B., & Rohr, U. (2015). *Jugendschutz im regulierten Cannabismarkt* (p. 7). Grundlagenpapier.

Still, it quickly becomes clear when looking at the FOPH web archive that the Swiss regulatory strategy has a solid scientific foundation. This is important for at least two reasons: First of all, every political project of such scope and far-reaching social consequences as cannabis legalization should have a solid scientific foundation. Second of all, it was already mentioned how the drug control regime is sensitive to scenarios where formal laws and what is actually implemented drift too far apart. The suspicion that Switzerland might use a formal scientific experiment to introduce the regulation of cannabis through the backdoor seems clearly unfounded. Moreover, a closer look at the conceptualization of the pilot trials also reinforces the impression that central questions of cannabis regulation are to be investigated in an unbiased and open-ended manner.[22] Four overarching priorities form the core of the project: First, it is about promoting individual and public health. Second is the protection of public order and the reduction of crime. Thirdly, the protection of youth plays a central role, and fourthly, there is an increase in prosperity and social justice. While the first three points are well known, the fourth priority deserves a closer look.

Switzerland's Previous Experiences With Cannabis Regulation

How does Switzerland intend to increase prosperity and social justice through the legalization of recreational cannabis? While the obvious answer would point to the benefits of an emerging cannabis industry and tax revenues, the Swiss regulatory strategy is more nuanced. The report points to experiences from other countries showing that profit-oriented actors quickly gain influence and want to influence the regulatory framework in their favor. 'Therefore, despite Switzerland's liberal tradition, it seems appropriate to explore moderate alternatives to a commercial approach. In addition, issues of social justice and equity as well as supply chain monitoring are of particular importance'.[23] The Swiss have very good reasons for being skeptical about commercial cannabis providers, and a preference is for so-called non-commercial providers such as cannabis social clubs, non-profit shops, and, to a limited extent, dispensaries. One of the many reasons for this skepticism can be found in the past more precisely in a memorable 'social experiment' that was conducted in Switzerland about 20 years ago.

At the beginning of the noughties, the Swiss had already considered legalizing cannabis for recreational use. But after only two years, the spook was

22 Zwicky, R., Brunner, P., Caroni, F., & Kübler, D. (2021). *A research agenda for the regulation of non-medical cannabis use in Switzerland* (Zurich Policy and Evaluation Studies No. 20, p. 21). Department of Political Science.

23 Zwicky et al., 2021, 22.

over and the project was scrapped. What had happened? At the beginning of 2000, the Swiss government prepared a bill based on the Dutch coffee shop model.[24] However, in order to avoid the Dutch backdoor problem, not only the possession and sale of small quantities were to be tolerated but also the production of larger quantities, provided that producers and retailers submitted to strict control by the police and the Ministry of Agriculture. In addition, a strict age limit of 18 years or older was applied.

However, the Swiss government had apparently underestimated the dynamics these plans would set off. Quickly, structures for the production, distribution, and sale of cannabis emerged before the legalization law was even passed. Within a short time, a quasi-legal market for cannabis was formed, with more than 400 sales outlets throughout the country.[25] A whole series of parallel scientific studies made the effects of this quasi-legalization visible with sobering results. Particularly interesting are so-called fake-client studies conducted by the well-known Swiss criminologist Martin Killias and his team. In these studies, young test buyers were sent out to purchase a small amount of cannabis. In 29 of the selected 50 test shops, they received cannabis without being asked for proof of age. In only five of the shops, proof of age was requested, and although this proved the test buyers to be minors, they were nevertheless sold cannabis in three shops. The potency of the cannabis sold was also relatively strong, with an average THC content of over 15%.[26] These many undesirable side effects ensured that the Swiss parliament finally stopped the amendment of the Narcotics Law in September 2003 and prohibition was reinstated.

An Almost Great Approach to Regulation

The Swiss failed attempt to legalize cannabis is a great example to demonstrate the need for solid strategies before the first regulatory steps are taken. Too much is at stake to leave cannabis to the mechanisms of a free market. Switzerland has drawn its conclusions from the debacle and seems determined to do things right this time. The introduction of pilot studies clearly is the right way to go from both a scientific and legal point of view. Just like the Dutch plan, this approach takes a middle way between rushing a full legalization of the soft drug with potential negative effects for society and remaining stuck in a prohibitive system out of fear that once the genie is out of the bottle, it will be difficult or even impossible to reinstate the ban. Pilot studies are designed to test what does work and what does not. Above all, the

24 Killias, M. (2011). Do drug policies affect cannabis markets? A natural experiment in Switzerland, 2000–10. *European Journal of Criminology*, 8(3), 171–186.

25 Killias, 2011, 173.

26 Killias, 2011, 176.

clear commitment to exclude commercial interests from the regulatory process as far as possible deserves attention. Experiences with Big Tobacco and the alcohol industry have taught us how difficult regulation can be once these industries have gathered sufficient power to systematically lobby lawmakers. Particularly worrying would be a market dynamic described by Caulkins et al. where the cannabis industry is incentivized to create and sustain intensive consumption patterns among users. This dynamic frequently observed in the alcohol business is based on the logic that the relatively few heavy users account for the lion's share of consumption. Hence, it must be expected that product design, pricing, and marketing will specifically aim to create as much heavy use as possible.[27]

However, like the Dutch approach, the Swiss model encounters the same problem: How will regulation continue after the experiment is concluded? We already saw that while pilot studies may be compliant with international law, this does not mean that a regulatory model based on these pilots will be. While breaking international law is serious for the Dutch as well as for the Germans, this might be less of an issue for the Swiss with their long tradition of neutrality. Not to forget that, so far, and as the examples of Canada and Uruguay will show, the consequences of breaking the international drug treaties seem neglectable.

Moreover, Switzerland is not a member state of the European Union which means that EU law is not directly applicable in the country. However, the situation is different with a view to the Schengen agreement, which was ratified by Switzerland who became a member of the Schengen area in 2008. As we have seen, the Schengen agreement contains regulations banning cannabis from signatory states. While EU member states in violation of these rules run the risk of being sued before the Court of Justice of the European Union, the situation for Switzerland is somewhat different. In the association agreement concerning the implementation of the Schengen Aquis between the EU and Switzerland, it is stated that in case of conflict with regard to the Schengen rules, a joint committee meeting at the ministerial level will set out to resolve the dispute.[28] If, however, a settlement is not reached, the regulation states that the entire agreement shall be terminated, effectively resulting in Switzerland leaving Schengen. It remains open as to how likely such a scenario really would be.

27 Caulkins et al., 2016, 112–113.

28 See Article 10 of the Abkommen zwischen der Schweizerischen Eidgenossenschaft, der Europäischen Union und der Europäischen Gemeinschaft über die Assoziierung dieses Staates bei der Umsetzung, Anwendung und Entwicklung des Schengen-Besitzstands. Abgeschlossen am 26. Oktober 2004. https://www.fedlex.admin.ch/eli/cc/2008/113/de.

Portugal: A Shining Example With a Few Shadows

Besides the Netherlands and Switzerland, there is another European country that is particularly interesting in terms of drug policy: Portugal. For many, the country is considered the most modern and progressive when it comes to drugs in general and cannabis in particular. Legalization advocates from all over the world see in the Portuguese concept a kind of blueprint for a successful, pragmatic, and humane drug policy.[29] Of particular note is the fact that in the 1990s, the country struggled with epidemic levels of drug abuse, particularly heroin, and the side effects of drug-related deaths, crime, and HIV/AIDS. But Portugal managed to turn the tide and is today above average in terms of drug use compared to the rest of Europe.[30] How did Portugal manage to achieve this? The answer is radical drug policy reform and a national drug strategy with a focus on decriminalization of all drugs and treatment of users.

Ex Course: Decriminalization vs. Legalization

If something is not prohibited, it does not automatically mean that it is permitted – at least not in the sense of criminal law. While this may sound like legal hair-splitting, it is of quite some relevance. Wrong parking is generally not a crime, i.e., punishable by criminal law. But that does not mean that it is allowed. On the contrary, anyone who parks incorrectly risks an administrative fine. The situation is similar when it comes to the decriminalization of drugs. The UN defines this as a process through which an offence is reclassified from 'criminal' to 'non-criminal' through legislative action; while the behavior remains an offence, it may be addressed through other means than criminal law.[31] Those other means can be administrative sanctions like fines, treatment mandates, or other civil sanctions. In case of wrong parking, this would be a parking ticket with a fine to be paid. For legal laymen, the difference between those two is often difficult to comprehend, as monetary fines are also a substantial part of criminal law. Legally, however, there are some differences, for example, in the possibilities of legal protection and the question of who is allowed to impose fines under administrative law and who is allowed to punish crimes by imposing financial penalties. Generally speaking, administrative offenses are minor violations of the law, such as parking offenses,

29 Rêgo, X., Oliveira, M. J., & Lameira, C. (2021). 20 years of Portuguese drug policy – developments, challenges and the quest for human rights. *Substance Abuse, Treatment and Prevention Policy*, 16(59), 7.

30 See EMCDDA. (2019). *Portugal country drug report 2019*. https://www.emcdda.europa.eu/publications/country-drug-reports/2019/portugal_en. An exception is the use of opioids, where Portugal is among the top five consumer countries.

31 In the UNODC, 2022, 28.

which are not so serious that one would want to burden the police, the public prosecutor's office, and the courts with them. Hence, decriminalization does not only seem to be an ideal instrument to deal with minor drug offenses in a flexible and quick way. The UN also explicitly considers it to be in line with the drug control regime under international law, and so does EU law.

Decriminalization of drugs has to be strictly distinguished from legalization. According to the UN, the latter usually refers to 'the regulation and commercialization of controlled drugs, such as cannabis, for non-medical and non-scientific purposes entailing no penalty (whether criminal, administrative, civil or otherwise) for production, manufacture, export, import and distribution of the drug'. The two concepts are often used interchangeably due to a misunderstanding of the more technical legal concept of decriminalization. The logical error lies in the assumption that everything that is not prohibited by criminal law must be permitted by law. Hence, the second part of the UN definition stating that decriminalized behavior remains an offense is overlooked. Or it is purposefully ignored by proponents of progressive drug policies for the reason that decriminalization, although considered a step in the right direction, suffers from serious shortcomings. For example, while it normalizes the use of certain drugs, it does not offer legal means to obtain these drugs. Decriminalization has almost zero impact on reducing the black market; more likely are adverse effects by helping it grow. Technically, decriminalization does little to help control the quality of drugs, protect the youths, or lead to tax revenues from drug production. Often, decriminalization only ratifies practices already in place, and hence, changing the law has little to no impact at all on the situation.[32]

The Portuguese Approach to Decriminalization

The Portuguese approach is designed to make the most out of decriminalizing drugs while remaining in compliance with international and European law. In order to achieve this, the legislators went to great lengths and made some rather unique legislative choices. The Portuguese system is not based on the distinction between hard and soft drugs like the Dutch one. All drugs, not only cannabis, but also hard drugs like cocaine and even heroin, are included in the decriminalization. Public and private consumption, acquisition, and possession have been decriminalized as long as the amount does not exceed the individual need for ten days. Such a ten-day ration corresponds in practice to a daily dose of 0.1 g of heroin, 0.1 g of ecstasy, 0.1 g of amphetamines, 0.2 g of cocaine, or 2.5 g of cannabis.[33] At first sight, the amounts don't seem

32 Caulkins et al., 2016, 172.

33 Caitlin, E. H., & Stevens, A. (2010). What can we learn from the Portuguese decriminalization of illicit drugs? *The British Journal of Criminology*, 50(6), 999–1022, 1004.

significant and are, with regards to cannabis, seemingly lower than what is tolerated in the Netherlands and Germany. However, by introducing the ten-day amount an average individual would use, the actually decriminalized amounts are ten times higher. It is an interesting example of a simple yet impractical legal solution to formally comply with international law. Formally, very small amounts that clearly fall within the amount for personal consumption are decriminalized, while in reality, consumers can possess up to 25 grams without fearing legal consequences simply for the reason that the law assumes (or fictionalizes) the amount is used over the course of ten days. However, the ten days are entirely fictional, and there is no way for the police to control if the amount is really used over this period of time or if the user possesses 25 different grams of cannabis the next day and so on. We will later come back to this legal trick the Portuguese came up with when the German approach is discussed.

More decisive for the Portuguese model is the idea of instead of differentiating between soft and hard drugs, they differentiate between users and dealers. The former are to be regarded as patients who must be offered support. The latter, on the other hand, will continue to be punished and handed over to the judicial system. In practice, users caught with small amounts of cannabis are not punished by criminal law but rather may get a citation to appear before a Commission for the Prevention of Drug Abuse (CDTs, in the Portuguese acronym). These consist of several people, including lawyers, social workers, and medical experts. The commissions can impose a range of sanctions, including community service, fines, and even temporary professional bans. Primarily, however, the aim is not to deter but to detect addiction risks at an early stage and to refer vulnerable users to medical services. Consumers are encouraged to become abstinent from drugs and, if necessary, start a therapy. The latter is voluntary, but appearing before the commission is obligatory.

This is one of the points of criticism of the Portuguese system. Apart from the enormous effort and the high costs, the system may not be as effective as hoped for other reasons. As Rego et al. point out, 90% of the cases that end up before a commission concern people who are not at risk of addiction.[34] The vast majority (83%) of those are cannabis users whose health risks are already low. The authors speak of a paradox that despite decriminalization, an increasing number of people are criminally sanctioned – including fines, jail time, and a combination of both – for drug use, making it the most punished offense right after drug dealing. While until 2008, sentences for drug use were almost nonexistent, a shift occurred mainly attributed to the jurisprudence of courts slowly softening the intended policy.

34 Rêgo et al., 2021, 5.

In conclusion, Portugal's middle path is drug policy-wise well conceptualized, and the successful impact has been clearly visible. The focus on treatment and harm reduction is unique but also complex and expensive. The policy is carefully designed to formally comply with international law. From the outset, Portugal's 'Sonderweg' and deviation from the strict prohibitive system prescribed by the European Union was based on the exception contained in EU law which allows national policies to depart from prohibitive principles for prevention and treatment of addictions.[35] As the situation in the country eased in the following years, the prohibitive spirit returned, driven not by policy change but by an increasingly rigid jurisdiction and law enforcement.

Cannabis in Canada and Uruguay: Open Breach of International Treaties

Until now, the analytical focus was on Europe with its complex interplay of international, European, and national regulations on drug policies. When it comes to cannabis regulations, it is, however, very much worth casting a light on policy models implemented beyond the borders of the European continent. More precisely at Canada and Uruguay. For legalization advocates, these two countries are no less than lighthouses in the rough waters of international cannabis prohibition. In both countries, cultivation, trade, and consumption of recreational cannabis is fully legalized. In 2013, Uruguay became the first country ever to regulate cannabis for non-medical purposes. Politically, legalization was initiated by the president and government officials (the public remained rather skeptical) and was justified with the protection of human health and human rights. Possible conflicts with international law were brushed off with the argument that in the event of a conflict between human rights obligations and international requirements of drug control, Uruguay was obliged to give priority to its human rights obligations.[36]

Canada argued in a very similar way when the so-called Cannabis Act came into force on 17 October 2018. There, too, the position was that the project was in line with international law. However, the then Canadian Minister of Foreign Affairs Chrystia Freeland rowed back before the Canadian Senate in May 2018. She conceded that cannabis legalization would violate 'certain obligations with respect to cannabis under the three UN drug conventions', adding, 'We need to address this openly'. Freeland reiterated that the Canadian government is 'definitely open to working with treaty partners to find solutions that take into account different approaches to cannabis within

35 See the Joint Declaration in the Final Act Schengen Implementation Convention which is discussed in Chapter 4.

36 Walsh, J., & Jelsma, M. (2019). Regulating drugs: Resolving conflicts with the UN drug control treaty system. *Journal of Illicit Economies and Development*, 1(3), 266–271, 268.

the international framework'.[37] Which solutions specifically she had in mind remains open until today.

The reaction of the UN, and in particular its Narcotics Control Board (INCB), was not very enthusiastic about the two countries' initiatives. In 2013 in a press release, INCB President Raymond Yans expressed surprise that Uruguay had knowingly decided to violate the universally agreed and internationally approved legal provisions of the 1961 Single Convention on Narcotic Drugs.[38] Yans was even more explicit with regard to Canada's legalization initiative. He accused the country of contributing to the weakening of the international legal framework for drug control and undermining the international order.[39] The Canadian Cannabis Act must be annulled, the panel demanded.

The critical stance of the board whose core task is to monitor the signatory states to ensure that they comply with the obligations of the drug control treaties has not changed over the years. For example, in its 2020 report, it expresses concern that several countries in Europe have taken steps to legalize recreational use in violation of the provisions of the international drug control treaty.[40]

Regulation of Cannabis in Canada and Uruguay

Apart from the harsh headwind Canada and Uruguay faced for their initiatives, it is worth having a closer look at their regulatory models. While their justifications and aims were similar the regulatory approaches in both countries differed considerably. In Canada, the Cannabis Act applies nationwide, but the individual provinces are allowed to largely determine for themselves how they regulate cannabis. This has led to very different regulatory models in the country. While in some provinces, the state fully controls cultivation and sales, elsewhere, private cannabis companies are in the driver's seat.[41] For example, the age of sale for cannabis can vary depending on the province: While in Alberta the minimum age is 18, this is 19 in Ontario and 21 in Quebec.

37 Walsh & Jelsma, 2019.

38 United Nations Information Service: Uruguay is breaking the international conventions on drug control with the cannabis legislation approved by its congress. https://incb.org/documents/Publications/PressRelease/PR2013/press_release_111213.pdf.

39 Quoted from Walsh & Jelsma, 2019, 268.

40 INCB Report 2020, 96. https://www.incb.org/incb/en/publications/annual-reports/annual-report-2020.html.

41 Zobel, F., & Schmidhauser, V. (2021). *Literature review on the impact of cannabis legalisation in the USA, Canada and Uruguay*. Sucht Schweiz.

Uruguay, on the other hand, has introduced a strictly state-controlled model throughout the country. Consumers are obliged to register with the state cannabis agency (Instituto de Regulación y Control del Cannabis), and there are only three legal ways to obtain cannabis: Growing the plants by oneself, joining one of the cannabis clubs, or buying it at the pharmacy. Quantities are strictly controlled by a fingerprint system. Members of the social clubs can obtain up to 40 grams per month while home growers may have no more than six female plants and produce a maximum of 480 grams of cannabis per year. In dispensaries, up to 40 grams per month can be purchased.[42]

The results of the Uruguayan model are still rather mixed ten years after legalization. A recent study from 2022 concluded that about 29% of cannabis users have officially registered a requirement to legally obtain the soft drug. Hence two thirds of users continue to buy cannabis on the black market or on the so-called grey market, i.e., as unregistered users from legal sources. Although the study demonstrates that, at least among regular users, the black-market demand has decreased by almost half, it also shows that even many of the registered users still use the black market. Thus, legalization has not only led to a coexistence of the black and the legal market but also created a new grey market.[43] One can only speculate about the reasons for this. On the one hand, the authors of the aforementioned study assume that many consumers shy away from registration, which also involves the collection of personal data. On the other hand, it could play a role that legals cannabis is limited in its potency to 9% THC content, and stronger weed is only available on the black market. The growers' clubs (there are said to be over 200 in the country) are limited in accepting new members, which has led to long waiting lists and thus continues to push consumers into the black market. While in Canada local conditions such as, for example, the availability of legal cannabis in rural areas play a significant role for black market developments this does seems not to be the case in Uruguay as the study concedes: Data were collected in Montevideo, the capital, where there is no shortage of legal ways to obtain cannabis.

With regards to Canada, it is difficult to draw a generalized picture of the situation, since experiences can be quite different in the various provinces, depending on the regulatory model. However, the Cannabis Survey, which is conducted annually by the Canadian Ministry of Health, gives a clear picture of the development of consumption since legalization.[44] It shows that the feared increase in cannabis use among adolescents and young adults has not

42 Queirolo, R., Álvarez, E., Sotto, B., & Cruz, J. M. (2022). How high-frequency users embraced cannabis regulation in Uruguay. *Journal of Drug Issues 2023*, 53(4), 519–535, 521.

43 Queirolo et al., 2022.

44 The data are available at the following link. https://www.canada.ca/en/health-canada/services/drugs-medication/cannabis/research-data/canadian-cannabis-survey-2022-summary.html#s4.

occurred or that use has even decreased. In 2017, i.e., one year before legalization, 41% of Canadians in this age group stated that they had smoked pot in the last 12 months; in 2022, only 37% had done so. Overall, the representative survey displays a slight increase from 22% of Canadians having used cannabis for non-medical purposes in the past 12 months to 26% in 2023. While in 2022, 48% of the respondents stated that they acquire cannabis exclusively from legal or licensed sources, this number rose to 69% in 2024. Apparently, price, convenience, and potency play important roles for the one-third of consumers who still prefer illegal cannabis.

The bottom line for Uruguay and Canada is that the two pioneers have had mixed experiences so far. While consumption patterns have changed only marginally in both countries, the black market has remained stable in Uruguay. In Canada, however, it seems that a dynamic has unfolded, and we can observe growing successes in curbing the black market.

Cannabis in the USA: The Land of Contradictions

To finish this chapter, with a brief analysis of the situation in the US, it is, in a way, like coming full circle: It was from here that the hippie movement, and with it cannabis, conquered the youth cultures of the world in the '70s. It was here that the War on Drugs was conceived and taken out into the world to recapture the drug. The country was one of the first to legalize cannabis for medical purposes. As of the beginning of 2024, in 24 states as well as DC, cannabis is legal for recreational purposes, including California, Colorado, and New York. On a federal level, however, cannabis and everything related to it, from growing and selling down to possessing small amounts of medical marijuana, remain completely illegal under federal law.[45] This contradiction has its roots in the US federal system, which shares a lot of commonalities with German federalism. According to the US Supreme Court, the states cannot actually legalize cannabis as this would require changing federal laws when, indeed, the Constitution's so-called Supremacy Clause dictates that federal law takes precedence over conflicting state laws.[46]

However, since the implementation of prohibition and law enforcement is a matter for the states and their law enforcement agencies under common law, some have made use of the option to legalize cannabis. The federal administration under President Obama made a deliberate decision to accept state-regulated cannabis industries and even actively paved the way by adapting laws to simplify business operations.[47] Nevertheless, it is worth pointing

45 Caulkins et al., 2016, 242.

46 Congressional Research Service. (2024). *Legal consequences of rescheduling Marijuana*. Legal Sidebar. https://crsreports.congress.gov/product/pdf/LSB/LSB11105.

47 Caulkins et al., 2016, 244.

out that individuals and organizations involved in the marijuana industry may be confronted with a variety of collateral consequences arising from federal prohibition, ranging from money laundering violations for businesses, exclusion from government benefits, and adverse immigration consequences for individuals.[48]

The contradiction has also created an interesting situation with regard to international law. Formally, one could argue the US is in compliance with international drug control treaties, since it adheres to the prohibitive rules. The US states might be in violation of the drug treaties, but since they are not signatory states and, hence, not directly bound by the regulations, this might be negligible. However, given the fact that the US, over decades, was a fierce supporter and driver of drug prohibition, including that of cannabis, the change of mind did not sit well with the INCB whose president reminded the US to ensure the implementation of the treaties on the entirety of its territory.[49]

The Invisible Hand of the Free Cannabis Market

Besides these legal aspects, there are some societal issues in the US that are worth mentioning. In the beginning, legalization was strongly driven by the idea of social justice. Ethnic minorities, in particular, were supposed to benefit from the legal cannabis business – i.e., those who suffered most from strict criminal prosecution in the past. Today, little remains of these noble goals. Large cannabis corporations largely divide the legal business among themselves. Cannabis and its legalization remain controversial today. On one side are conservative activists and religious groups, but also skeptical scientists and journalists who never tired of pointing out the dangers of cannabis use.[50] On the other side, think tanks financed by powerful personalities like George Soros have pushed millions into advocating for legalization. For a long time, this legalization movement, driven by a political agenda including social justice issues, dominated the societal discourse. Today, cannabis lobby organizations with clear commercial interests have taken over.[51]

After the first legalization initiatives, a kind of gold rush broke out with hundreds of small companies appearing, claiming their piece of the marijuana pie and the billion-dollar business. Initially prizes were rising, followed by a steep decline. In California, for example, the US Mecca for cannabis, many of the so-called dispensaries of small cannabis farmers have had to go out of

48 Congressional Research Service, 2024.

49 Caulkins et al., 2016, 248.

50 Berenson, A. (2019). *Tell your children: The truth about Marijuana, mental illness and violence*. Free Press.

51 Caulkins et al., 2016, 196–197.

business, even though the Californian climate is optimal for growing quality cannabis. Government regulation and high taxation, as well as competition from cheap black-market cannabis, have forced start-ups into bankruptcy. What remains are large-scale cannabis farmers with huge, highly efficient greenhouses and financially strong investors or pharmaceutical companies behind them who divide up the legal market among themselves. The profiteers are an economic elite and not the minority communities that have suffered in the past under the rigid cannabis laws.

These developments have led to the question of whether state regulation is a driver of these problems. However, new markets are often subject to a consolidation phase. It just takes a while for stable and sustainable structures to establish themselves. Ultimately, this is for the good of the consumer and the less the state intervenes in a regulatory way, the faster and better this process can take place. Still, cannabis is not a normal consumer product, and there are good reasons why the control and taxation of cannabis is higher than for other consumer products. For example, the appearance of edibles, often in the form of candy, jelly bears, or lollipops, is a very worrying development not only because the dosage is hard to control but also because the number of young children admitted to hospitals with poisoning has risen sharply since 2017.[52] Some studies have also found evidence that road safety is affected by an increasing number of accidents under the influence of cannabis.[53] Social acceptance of cannabis legalization stands and falls with the cushioning of the social costs via the lever of taxation of those who profit most from it, hence, the industry behind the drug. However, the cannabis market is also unique in that competition comes not only from market participants but also from a huge black market. Its protagonists, however, have no tax burden, do not have to pay social contributions for their employees, and do not have to comply with any other standards.

Discussions in Europe about the legalization of cannabis often focus on models with state monopolies and strict regulations where the state either directly produces and supplies the drug or at least keeps a firm control on private actors taking over that role. This might be due to the strong paternalistic traditions on the continent and the skepticism towards the invisible hand of the free market. In the US, different traditions are cherished, and developments in the emerging cannabis market seem to corroborate these. While there is much to learn from the US, the legal limbo created by contradictory

52 Marit, S. T., Nemanich, A., & Wahl, M. (2023). Pediatric edible cannabis exposures and acute toxicity: 2017–2021. *Pediatrics*, 151(2).

53 French, M. T., Zukerberg, J., Lewandowski, T. E., Piccolo, K. B., & Mortensen, K. (2022) Societal costs and outcomes of medical and recreational Marijuana policies in the United States: A systematic review. *Medical Care Research and Review*, 79(6), 743–771.

federal and state laws is far from being an ideal ground for an effective regulatory model.

Conclusion

The title of this chapter is misleading: It only looked at very few examples of cannabis regulation from around the globe, while many countries that would have been worth taking a closer look at have been left out. Jamaica, for example, implemented some interesting approaches to cannabis, and so has Thailand. Within the EU, the Czech Republic is at the forefront at pushing back on prohibition. So are Malta and Luxembourg, two rather small EU countries that recently have been breaking new ground in cannabis policies. Legalization advocates speak of a ‘green wave’ that is sweeping across the world and encompassing more and more countries. While this metaphor is enticing, it only tells a part of the truth. While a number of countries are discussing cannabis regulation, and some have moved towards more liberal approaches, this is far from the majority. In the same way, there are many countries that are not breaking new ground in drug policy or have even become stricter recently in their approach to drugs and, more specifically, to cannabis. Russia and Saudi Arabia are the only two countries that are a little tolerant towards drugs in all forms. In Europe, Sweden has implemented a zero-tolerance policy towards all forms of drugs. Even alcohol is sold there only under strict state supervision. The neighboring country Denmark with Christiania, the world-famous hippie enclave in the middle of Copenhagen where cannabis was sold freely, has only recently rowed back on its liberal approach. The enclave was infiltrated by increasingly violent organized criminals, leaving inhabitants no choice but to curb the selling of the soft drug.

Little signs of a green wave can be found at the shores of the United Kingdom, and this is despite the fact that the renowned Kings College in London is one of the leading institutions in cannabis research worldwide. The researchers there study the effects of cannabis mainly from a neurological perspective and have earned a reputation as conservative warnings against cannabis use.[54]

In this respect, the purpose of this analysis was merely to highlight interesting traits of different policy approaches. The aim was not to give an overall assessment of the regulations and their implementation, as this would be impossible, at least in such a limited space. The approaches are too diverse, and their implementation is too different. Above all of them is the long shadow cast by international treaties, limiting the room for maneuvering. Only Canada and, to a lesser extent, Uruguay have so far opted for an open violation

54 Berenson, 2019.

of the drug control treaties, met with little enthusiasm by the INCB but with equally little consequences.

Within the EU the situation is different. The ambition of a number of member states to interpret the EU treaties broadly and even look for loopholes seems great. The Netherlands and Portugal are two examples whose creativity in that matter have stretched the regulations considerably. In the case of the Netherlands and its Wietexperiment, this search for new paths in drug policies continues even if, from time to time, it seems to lose direction: Recently, prominent voices have been heard proposing similar pilot studies for cocaine ultimately aiming at regulating harder drugs as well. While the motivation behind this may be the urgent need to gain back control of organized crime, the suggestion itself manifests the perhaps greatest fear of that skeptical or openly opposing cannabis regulation: The risk that the green wave might cause a dambreak.

Leaving the question aside of how realistic such demands are from a legal and political point of view, the Dutch cannabis policy may have been unconventional, to say the least, and stretching the EU rules quite a bit. This is something the country has in common with Portugal. However, both EU member states have taken considerable care and gone to great lengths to implement their drug policies in a way that remains in compliance with EU laws. So far, the EU Commission has remained silent, tacitly accepting these approaches. The question is whether this will change in the future. What will most certainly remain unchanged are the EU rules themselves. At least at the time of this writing, there are no initiatives on the horizon that would further develop the EU treaties with regard to drug prohibition. Those who contemplate real change have to wait for the outcome of the Wietexperiment, hoping it will provide empirical data able to prompt a rethink among Brussels bureaucrats. However, depending on the outcome and the quality of the collected data, the pendulum might also swing back toward prohibition.

6 Europe's Cannabis Dilemma

Introduction

Right after Easter 2023, German Minister of Health Karl Lauterbach presented his plans for legalizing cannabis in Germany. At this point, the original plans of a 'total legalization', including a comprehensively regulated cannabis market, were considerably downsized to what was called a 'legalization light'. The term itself is a euphemism as the law, in essence, is a partial decriminalization and is far away from a real legalization. This light version consists of two pillars, the first of which is a bill to decriminalize the possession of up to 25 grams of cannabis. In addition, so-called *Anbauvereinigungen*, i.e., cannabis growers' associations with up to 500 members, will be allowed, with each member being able to bring in up to three female cannabis plants. The second pillar then provides for regional model projects with pilots for commercial cultivation and supply chains, as we already know from similar projects in the Netherlands and Switzerland. Before having a closer look at this regulatory model, however, the question arises as to what happened to the high-flying plans of the German government of fully legalizing cannabis. Why were these plans significantly downsized to a partial decriminalization?

To fully comprehend this political process, it is worth having a quick look at the recent evolution of the bill. It was already mentioned in Chapter 2 that the first serious attempt to fully legalize cannabis was undertaken by the German Green Party in 2015. A bill for a so-called cannabis control law was introduced to the Bundestag, which, after traveling through various committees, was finally rejected by the conservative majority in 2020. While the bill had died, the idea of treading new paths in the German cannabis policies survived. It hibernated until 2021, when the legalization plans, to the surprise of many, had made it into the coalition agreement of the newly elected German government.

Soon after, the German health minister declared the legalization of cannabis as one of his priorities. He wanted to tackle the mammoth task in close coordination with the Ministry of the Interior, the Ministry of Justice, and even the Ministry of Agriculture. But despite these concentrated efforts, over

DOI: 10.4324/9781003503439-7

a year later, there was no draft bill, but merely the already mentioned *Eckpunktepapier*, which consisted of a rough outline and some conceptualizing notes on a possible bill.[1] This framework paper was sent to the EU Commission in October 2022 with a friendly request to share their thoughts on this, particularly if this complies with EU law. The response of the Commission was reserved, to say the least, not so much in terms of the legalization plans themselves – the experts at the Commission were, of course, fully aware of the legal complexities of such an endeavor – but more with regards to the form of the request.

Generally, it is not unusual for the EU Commission to assess the conformity of draft bills from member states with EU regulations. For this, the Commission provides a notification procedure, a formal assessment of any draft technical regulation before its adoption. During a standstill period of three months, the Commission (and other member states) can examine the bill's text and submit a detailed opinion.[2] This procedure, of course, requires a finished draft bill including all the details of the envisioned regulation. A rough sketch of the draft bill is not sufficient, especially when it involves a complex undertaking such as the regulation of cannabis with far-reaching societal implications. As to why the why the German health minister did not provide a finished draft bill to the EU Commission one can only speculate. One reason may have been that when looking closely into the relevant EU regulations, it must have become clear to the experts in the ministries that the endeavor of legalizing cannabis was more complicated than initially thought. Why then invest time and effort into drafting a full bill only for it to fail the notification procedure after all? The hope might have been that the EU Commission would be willing to give a thumbs down or up for the overall plans, and only in the latter case would the ministry have drafted a full bill. Others, like Markus Lanz, the TV show host from the introduction of this book, speculated that Lauterbach had hoped for a rejection of the Commission so that he could cancel the legalization plans and blame the Commission for burying the bill.

Either way, the EU Commission did not officially react to the plans, neither green lighting nor rejecting the German plans, thereby putting the ball back in the field of the German health minister. One of his options would have been to flee forward and enact a full legalization bill and formally submit it for notification. Another option would have been to skip the notification procedure entirely and to enact the full bill. In cases of objections, the EU Commission would have been forced to initiate an infringement procedure against Germany. Then, the Court of Justice of the European Union would have to decide, and the procedure's outcome would lay in the hands of the judges. This would

1 German Government. (2022). *Eckpunktepapier der Bundesregierung zur Einführung einer kontrollierten Abgabe von Cannabis an Erwachsene zu Genusszwecken* (p. 2). German Government.

2 See EU Directive 2015/1535.

have provided the chance to get a clear and definitive verdict on the question of cannabis legalization in the European Union.

However, the German government was reluctant to take this risk for reasons that had little to do with cannabis but with what easily can be called the biggest regulatory disasters of contemporary German history. In 2019, in the case C-591/17, *Republic of Austria v Republic of Germany*, the CJEU ruled that the German infrastructure toll for passenger vehicles discriminated against EU citizens. Germany had previously passed a law requiring all passenger cars using the German autobahn to pay a toll, with the twist that German car owners could claim the toll back through their taxes. The CJEU rightly saw this as clear discrimination on grounds of nationality under Article 18 TFEU and struck down the German law. As if this wasn't bad enough, the German Ministry of Transportation had already commissioned a number of companies to set up the infrastructure to collect the toll. These had made considerable investments and sued the German state after the annulment of the law. Ultimately, German taxpayer almost paid ¬250 million in damages.[3]

Would a similar scenario have loomed with regard to cannabis legalization? Regarding the car toll, experts had warned early on that the plans would violate European rules. In the case of regulating cannabis, the situation was similar, and it was already discussed in Chapter 4 that EU regulations provide little wiggle room for member states to depart from an overall prohibitive system. The scale of the damage caused by a subsequent reversal of cannabis law would probably have been somewhat smaller. Nevertheless, growers and retailers would have made investments based on the legal validity of the law and may have accumulated considerable losses. Hence, the reluctance of the health minister to take such a risky path with the cannabis bill seems understandable. However, while previously only the skeptics of legalization had criticized the minister's plans, the supporters now joined in the criticism, describing the minister's approach as half-hearted, particularly in view of the bold initial announcements. It begs the question: Could all of this be foreseen and avoided beforehand? To find an answer, we need to take another look at the past and the scientific debate on cannabis in Germany.

The Father to the Thought

The wish is father to the thought. The famous proverb from Shakespeare's Henry IV insinuates that our hopes and dreams all too often influence our opinions and beliefs. Legal opinions and beliefs are no exception. If one recapitulates the German legal debate on cannabis legalization, one can easily get

3 DER SPIEGEL. (2023). Wissing prüft per Gutachten Regressforderung gegen Scheuer. *DER SPIEGEL*. https://www.spiegel.de/wirtschaft/maut-desaster-wissing-prueft-per-gutachten-regressforderung-gegen-scheuer-a-03683057-d7e4-4463-8476-796916b21ddc.

the impression that the international and EU legal framework offers plenty of room for member states to overcome prohibition. All it requires is a broad interpretation of the regulations and the political will to regulate the soft drug. In truth, however, we have seen that such an endeavor is much more complex. Legal scholars and scientists must point out these complexities, even if one's own political convictions or personal opinion may be different. The majority of researchers in the field of drug research seem to favor an end to cannabis prohibition. German scholars are no exception to this with the result that critical voices or voices suggesting more cautious approaches were scarce.

The result was that, just like Shakespeare's historical drama, the German plans to fully legalize cannabis over the time span of almost ten years followed a typical linear dramatic structure. It started with an exposition introducing the background of an initiative of over 122 legal experts and scientists in 2013 calling for the Narcotics Act to be reviewed with regard to the criminalization of cannabis.[4] The rising action was signified by a series of events, such as the draft of the cannabis control law introduced to the parliament by the Green Party in 2015. While the draft was initially rejected by parliament, the idea popped up again in the coalition agreement of 2021. Consumers, activists, and above all, the lobbyists of an emerging cannabis market rejoiced, with many believing that this is no less than the start signal for ending cannabis prohibition in Europe, maybe the entire world. The climax of the unfolding drama was reached when Germany's Minister of Health Karl Lauterbach declared legalization to be a top priority in 2022 and set out the framework for full legalization and a purely German cannabis market in his *Eckpunktepapier.* From there, things took a turn and quickly spiraled downwards to the rocky grounds of reality. The EU Commission neither officially opposed nor approved the German plans – at least not publicly. Either way, in April 2023, the resolution was the canceling of the original plans of fully legalizing cannabis. Instead, a new, scaled-down cannabis law was introduced.

How could the politicians follow the wrong track for so long with the result that, in the end, both the opponents and proponents were left unsatisfied with the outcome? One possible explanation would indeed be the strong power the wish may have over the thought. The German debate on drug reform was driven and nurtured by the confidence of legal scholars that legalization could be achieved if the political will was strong enough. This confidence has its roots within the complexities and traditions of German criminal law and doctrinal thinking – the latter described by the German term *Strafrechtsdogmatik* or criminal legal dogmatics. The term dogmatic originally stems from theology and refers to an official system of principles or teachings of a religion. Indeed, German doctrinal thinking in criminal law and Christian theology

4 The resolution can be accessed here. https://schildower-kreis.de/resolution-deutscher-strafrechtsprofessorinnen-und-professoren/.

seem to share a number of commonalities: The German Criminal Code is the center and main source of jurisprudence, and almost every year, more than a dozen commentaries on this code are published by respected scholars, sometimes already in their second or even third generation. Most of these commentaries are printed on thin Bible paper, can easily run to 3000 pages, and all have in common that they have more footnotes than readers. German criminal doctrinal thinking looks back on centuries-old traditions and the same world-class league in which German philosophy once played. Despite the fact that these times have long gone, German criminal law is still perceived by scholars, judges, and professionals as standing on the shoulders of giants, hence, ultimately being above other criminal legal systems, including the Anglo-American criminal justice system.[5] The problem is that on the shoulders of giants, it might be difficult to see what is happening on the ground.

This may serve as an explanation for the fact that many prominent German legal scholars voiced their support for cannabis legal reform while questions of international law and, more importantly, of EU law played a minor role. To a small extent, however, this ignorance may have its origins in a certain presumptuousness and German legal scholars putting the fragmented EU criminal regulations at the cat's table of legal doctrine. This has led to what a German legal scholar once called the 'confident provinciality' of German criminal law, and while this is a topic that is controversially discussed among German scholars, it seems as if there is little motivation to break out of this legal *Gemütlichkeit* or comfort zone.[6]

The Free Market Conundrum

An issue that was widely overlooked in the German debate about legalizing cannabis was the free market rules within the EU. In fact, while many of the EU regulations on cannabis may indeed provide some wiggle room for interpretation, the free market rules, in many respects, are sacrosanct to the EU Commission. It seems very plausible that these rules pose one, if not the main, obstacle to any member state's attempt to liberalize the domestic cannabis market.[7] The problem was first mentioned in a blog post and later taken up by

5 See for example the Ambos, K. (2020). Zukunft der deutschen Strafrechtswissenschaft. *Zeitschrift Internationale Strafrechtsdogmatik*, 2020(10), 452.

6 There is a decade old debate going on about this questionable superiority of German criminal doctrinal thinking. For those interested in the issue an excellent summary can be found in the special issue of the Zeitschrift für Internationale Strafrechtsdogmatik 10/2020 openly accessible online. www.zis-online.com.

7 For an in depth analysis see Hofmann, R. (2023). The 'total-legalization' of cannabis in Germany: Legal challenges and the EU free market conundrum. *European Journal of Crime, Criminal Law and Criminal Justice*, 31(2).

the *Eckpunktepapier* sketching out the legalization plans.[8] While legalizing cannabis in Germany and, hence, making it a legal product or commodity that can be freely traded in the domestic market, it was acknowledged that this would not change the fact that an international trade of cannabis for recreational purposes remained impossible. Hence, any import, export, or transit of recreational cannabis into, out of, or through Germany would still have to comply with EU law and, respectively, the customs laws.

Hence, while Germany would have redefined cannabis as an agricultural product, this would not have been the case for all of the remaining 27 EU member states. From a free-market perspective, Germany would have become an island for cannabis with no possibility of importing or exporting recreational cannabis through other states. The consequences of this are rather interesting: For example, a container of cannabis destined for German recreational use that lands in the port of Genoa in order to be further transported overland would be legally considered drug smuggling in Italy and all other transit countries. Since Italy is still bound by international law to prevent illegal trade, authorities may feel obliged to confiscate the product and prosecute the importers. As the same is true for most other countries in the world, cannabis shipments would, therefore, have to land in a German port directly from the country of origin without any stopover. The same would apply to recreational cannabis reaching Germany by air freight, for example, from Canada. But what if the airplane needs to make a stopover or emergency landing in another country? Would the pilots be arrested for drug smuggling? Which cargo company would take the risk?

The German legislature saw this problem and came up with a solution: National demand would have to be covered by production in Germany only.[9] The purely domestically cultivated cannabis would not only avoid the risk related to imported cannabis. It would also enable the German Cannabis Agency to implement and enforce strict quality control and security standards for German producers. However, from a free-market perspective, this solution of creating a purely domestic market within the European free market is less than ideal and would lead to complex follow-up problems. According to the case law of the CJEU, Article 34 TFEU prohibits all trading rules that are capable of hindering, directly or indirectly, actually or potentially, intra-community trade.[10] While there are some exceptions to this, a large body of CJEU case law on free market issues shows how complex and problematic the German plans may be. For example, in the 2007 *Rosengreen v Rikslageren* case, the CJEU ruled against the Swedish state monopoly that prohibited private individuals

8 Hofmann, R. (2022). *Welche Probleme das Cannabiskontrollgesetz lösen muss. Deutschlands Cannabis-Dilemma Teil 2*. https://verfassungsblog.de/cannabis-2/.

9 German Government, 2022, 11.

10 CJEU Judgment of 11 July 1974, Case 8–74 *Procureur du Roi v Benoît and Gustave Dassonville*.

from importing alcohol into Sweden from other EU member states. The Court found that the ban on the import of alcoholic beverages was unsuitable for protecting young people from the harmful effects of alcohol consumption and that the restriction on imports was, therefore, unjustified on the basis of Article 36 TFEU. The Swedish legislature solved the problem by allowing EU competitors to sell and deliver alcohol products ordered online in Sweden, hence, bypassing the state monopoly.[11] In a similar decision, the Court of Justice of the European Union ruled that a law prohibiting the import into Finland of ethyl alcohol with a strength of more than 80% was compatible with Article 36 TFEU because importers were only required to obtain a license.

Indeed, applied to cannabis, a licensing system for cannabis imports into Germany might be more in line with free market rules.[12] However, providing EU competitors with the possibility to obtain a license in order to export recreational cannabis to Germany is not mentioned in the regulatory framework. Maybe for good reasons, as such a system would be essentially redundant for at least two reasons. First of all, as long as no other EU member state has legalized cannabis producers cannot cultivate legally for the German recreational market with or without a license issued by the German state. Second of all, the CJEU clearly stated in the Josemans ruling, that cannabis is a prohibited substance under EU law. Hence, there is no right for EU citizens to buy this product, which, in consequence, would also apply to private individuals who wish to produce the product and import it into Germany. In conclusion, legalizing cannabis as an agricultural product in Germany but remaining an illicit product outside its borders and within the EU would have resulted in a perfectly shielded domestic cannabis market or what could be called a free market conundrum.[13]

The New German Cannabis Law

These complexities, obstacles, and legal risks ultimately resulted in the decision to abandon the plans of a full legalization of cannabis in Germany. Most of these challenges could have been known beforehand. This is a missed opportunity as a thorough analysis in advance would have enabled a coherent and balanced regulatory approach to cannabis. Hence, in 2023 and after consulting with the EU Commission, the German government had to return to the drawing board. In October 2023, German Health Minister Karl Lauterbach presented a new cannabis law, which the Bundestag approved in February of

11 CJEU Case C-170/04, 5 June 2007, *Klas Rosengren and Others v Riksåklagaren*.

12 CJEU Case C-434/04 from 28 September 2006, Criminal proceedings against Jan-Erik Anders Ahokainen and Mati Leppik where the CJEU considered import licensing of undernatured ethyl alcohol of over 80% into Finland as compliant with Article 36 TFEU.

13 Hofmann, 2023.

2024 and the Second Chamber, the Bundesrat approved it one month later. On 1 April 2024, the new cannabis law (CanG) came into force, while provisions pertaining to growers' associations came into force on 1 July 2024.[14]

While this cannabis law is a significantly watered-down version of what the government had originally planned, it still marks what could be called a new era in German cannabis policy. Given that the legislative process, which took more than two years, was characterized by controversy, missteps, and misunderstandings of the legal situation, it is not surprising that the result is a patchwork of compromises and subsequent adjustments. Still, the law, in many respects, is the first of its kind in the EU, so the legislature had few blueprints from which to draw. Nevertheless, there are some unconventional solutions to the problems posed by the prohibitive framework that are worth looking at. In the following section, some of the most important aspects of this cannabis law will be discussed in order to provide a general overview of how the regulations have been designed and where there is still room for improvement.

The central innovation of the Cannabis Act is that the soft drug is no longer regulated in the Narcotics Act but in two new laws, firstly the Consumption Cannabis Act (KCanG) and secondly the Medicinal Cannabis Act. Article 1 of the Consumption Cannabis Act regulates the handling of cannabis for recreational use, while Article 2 contains provisions on medical cannabis. Particularly relevant are the provisions of the Consumption Cannabis Act, Section 3 of which allows adults aged 18 and over to possess up to 25 grams of cannabis outside their own home for personal consumption. A quantity of 50 grams or three cannabis plants can be legally possessed at home. This even applies if the cannabis was purchased on the black market.[15] Cannabis may only be consumed in public if no schools, children's playgrounds, youth facilities, or sports facilities are within sight and not in pedestrian zones between 7 am and 8 pm (see §5). Violations can be punished as administrative offenses, and the federal states are free to impose fines (in accordance with § 36). Criminal provisions can be found in Section 34 KCanG, which follows the already familiar system and lists various behaviors that remain prohibited. For example, it is punishable if a person carries more than 30 grams of cannabis or stores more than 60 grams in their own home (§34 I No.1). However, it is still forbidden to distribute cannabis to other persons, even in minimal quantities. An early decision of a Bavarian court exemplifies how this may lead to rather curious

14 Bundesgesetzblatt Teil I 2024 Ausgegeben zu Bonn am 27. März 2024 Nr. 109, Gesetz zum kontrollierten Umgang mit Cannabis und zur Änderung weiterer Vorschriften (Cannabisgesetz – CanG).

15 Deutscher Bundestag. (2023). *Entwurf eines Gesetzes zum kontrollierten Umgang mit Cannabis und zur Änderung weiterer Vorschriften (Cannabisgesetz – CanG) Drucksache 20/8704* (p. 131). Deutscher Bundestag.

outcomes: A suspect had thrown 11 grams of cannabis onto the street while fleeing from the police. The court ruled that the man had illegally distributed the cannabis in public, an offense under §34 I No.10 of the law. If he had simply kept the cannabis with him, he would have gone unpunished.[16]

The (Social) Cannabis Clubs

While the regulations partly decriminalizing the possession and cultivation of cannabis for self-consumption are straightforward, the law gets more unconventional with regards to the so-called *Anbauvereinigungen* or cannabis clubs. Their purpose is to resolve the fundamental problem of how consumers who don't want to self-cultivate can be supplied with cannabis without having to resort to the black market.

Yet cannabis clubs are by no means new and certainly not an invention of the German government. Cannabis Social Clubs (CSCs) have existed in Europe since the 1990s and are associations of like-minded people who dedicate themselves to cannabis cultivation together in the clubhouse, share technical equipment and expertise, and consume the harvested product together in the private club premises. The clubs are not intended to be open to third persons or to be profit-oriented; the focus is on social aspects, usually limiting the number of members to a few dozen. The clubs consider themselves as a social movement towards fair and sustainable drug policies.[17] The CSCs have been particularly popular in Spain where, since 2002, and after a number of legal judgments concerning the decriminalization of self-cultivation, hundreds of such clubs were established.[18]

The legal foundation is the personal consumption and cultivation clause found in Article 2 I of the EU Framework Decision 2004/757/jha, which was discussed in length in Chapter 4. The idea behind the clubs is that it should not matter if one is cultivating cannabis plants for personal use at home or on the premises of a club closed to the public together with other like-minded club members. Indeed, a club run by professionals might provide an even safer environment for growing cannabis plants than a private apartment does. The non-commercial objective of the clubs ensures that aspects of drug trade and trafficking can be avoided.

Still, it is worth mentioning that a legal framework for these clubs does not exist in any EU member state, and hence, they cannot be considered legal. According to the EUDA, the clubs operate in a legal grey area at best and are

16 BayObLG, Beschluss vom 8.4.2024 – 203 StRR 39/24. https://openjur.de/u/2485257.html.

17 See at ENCOD.org.

18 Kilmer, B., Kruithof, K., Pardal, M., Caulkins, J. P., & Rubin, J. (2013). *Multinational overview of cannabis production regimes*. WODC.

regularly confronted with legal sanctions in almost all countries.[19] The compliance of this model with international and European law has been controversially discussed in the literature.[20] Cultivation within one's own four walls is only privileged based on the assumption that access for other persons can be limited and effectively controlled by the cultivator. This personal control, however, is lost when the plants are handed over to other persons (i.e., the club operators) and when other club members gain access to the plants. The member status of these other people is irrelevant with regard to the personal consumption privilege. Moreover, for law enforcement agencies, the clubs are difficult to distinguish from illegal cannabis plantations. It is almost impossible to check whether the individual plants can actually be attributed to real persons who then consume the harvest themselves or whether the weed ultimately ends up on the black market.

However, the regulatory framework, as planned in the KCanG §§11–30, sets out to overcome these weaknesses. Of the maximum of 500 members of an association, each member will be provided with not more than 50 grams of cannabis per month. The possibility of engaging external (commercial) providers, for example, crops or gardening services, is very restricted and completely forbidden for the cultivation and supply of the members with cannabis. The new law contains detailed regulations concerning location, structure, legal requirements, members, and documentation obligations in an attempt to establish a meticulous oversight over the clubs. Not surprisingly, one of the many concerns raised against the clubs was the question of how to handle the enormous effort of monitoring the clubs and effectively enforcing any violations of the law.

Despite these concerns, the true innovation of the *Anbauvereinigungen* is rather curious but is born out of necessity: The social part is removed from the clubs. What remains are mere associations for cultivation without the joint consumption of cannabis. The rationale behind this is that the legislature was eager to prevent establishments similar to the Dutch coffee shops where club members, as well as guests or third persons, completely unaffiliated with the club (e.g., tourists), would buy and consume cannabis. Clearly, the legislators attempted to avoid the impression that these clubs are de facto commercial dispensaries or distributors in an effort to comply with EU and international law. If this is convincing remains to be seen.

The aspects discussed so far form the first pillar of the Cannabis Act. However, the German legislature is also planning a second pillar, the

19 EMCDDA. (2016). *Models for the legal supply of cannabis: Recent developments*. Publications Office of the European Union.

20 Van Kempen, P. H., & Federova, M. (2019). *International law and cannabis: Regulation of cannabis cultivation for recreational use under the UN narcotic drugs conventions and the EU legal instruments in anti-drugs policy* (p. 216). Intersentia.

commercial production and distribution of cannabis, to be trialed in regional and time-limited pilot projects. These pilot projects are to be scientifically monitored to analyze the effects of a licensed trade of cannabis on health, child and youth protection, as well as the impact on the black market. These pilot projects are to be limited to a period of five years, although a precise timetable for the implementation of the projects is not yet available. However, experience from the Netherlands, where the starting signal for the pilot projects was delayed by years, gives rise to concerns that German studies are unlikely to materialize in the foreseeable future. Skeptics fear that a change of government after the next elections could put the projects on ice for good.

The Devils in the Details

So far, the analysis has focused on some of the most important regulatory concepts and guiding principles of Germany's new cannabis law. As often happens when it comes to implementing a new law, the devil is in the details. Not surprisingly, given the political struggles accompanying the legislative process, legal commentators seem to agree that there are a number of devils populating the cannabis law.[21] Some technical mistakes made during the enactment process could have been avoided. Others were so serious that they jeopardized the passing of the law as a whole.

Amnesties Under the Cannabis Law

One of the most controversial and, at the same time, most complex provisions of the law can be found in Article 13. It regulates by reference to §313 EGStGB an amnesty for people who were convicted for cannabis-related offenses before the new law came into force. Without going into too much detail at this point, this provision almost led to the entire law being rejected by the second chamber, the Bundesrat, where the 16 *Bundesländer* are represented. The core of the problem lies in the fact that while the cannabis law is drafted by the federal government, the Länder will be responsible for implementing and enforcing the law in practice. This can lead to tensions where the political interests of the federal government and the Länder constituting the federation may diverge. The cannabis law is a good example of this in many respects. The government, when drafting the law, had very consciously included an amnesty, meaning that people who have been convicted in the past but would not have been sentenced under the new law will be subsequently

21 Sobota, S. (2024). Das Cannabisgesetz als Zeitenwende im Drogenrecht. *Neue Jusristische Wochenschrift*, 2024(18), 1217; Oğlakcıoğlu, M., & Welke, P. (2024). Ganz seltsame Blüten . . . Das neue Cannabisgesetz im Überblick und der Versuch einer ersten Konsolidierung. *Kriminalpolitische Zeitschrift*, 9(3), 198.

acquitted or, when convicted for additional other crimes, receive a reduction of their sentence. Due to the ultima ratio function of criminal law and the restrictive impact on the individual freedom of prisoners, it was considered unacceptable that people would remain in prison for conduct that has turned legal in the world outside the prison walls.

However, this created a major problem for the Bundesländer and the subordinated public prosecutor's offices. Over 100,000 case files of people convicted in the past had to be re-examined to determine whether a conviction for cannabis had played a role, and if so, the sentence had to be reduced. Moreover, this had to be done in a timely manner as otherwise, the prosecutors could themselves be subjected to criminal liability for falsely imprisoning people. However, as the German justice system has been suffering from a digital backlog for years, and hence most case files are not digitalized, this review had to be carried out analog, i.e., by sweeping through thousands of files by hand. Hence, the states insisted for the amnesty rule to be either canceled or at least not applied retroactively to cases already concluded by threatening to block the law in the second chamber. However, the government did not give in. Ultimately and despite these concerns, the Bundesrat approved the cannabis law by a narrow majority at its meeting on 22 March 2024 and the law could come into force on 1 April 2024.

A Significant Amount of Cannabis and the German Federal Court

Only a few weeks after the cannabis law came into force, the German Federal Court of Justice (Bundesgerichtshof) issued in an unusually fast manner a decision with far-reaching consequences for the cannabis law and its enforcement. In Chapter 2 of this book, it was already discussed that German narcotics law imposes more severe penalties if prohibited behavior, such as trafficking, relates to a quantity of the prohibited substance that is of some significance and, hence, not a small amount (so-called *nicht geringe Menge*). What exactly constitutes a significant amount of a certain substance has been determined by the German Federal Court via case law. Accordingly, the threshold quantity of a narcotic is determined by its specific effects, such as the amount of a lethal dose or, if not lethal, a multiple of the average unit usually consumed.[22] With regards to cannabis and based on scientific findings dating back to the 1980s, the Federal Court of Justice had estimated that based on the dangerousness of cannabis, a quantity of 7.5 g THC active ingredient content qualifies as

22 BGH Beschluss vom 18. April 2024 – 1 StR 106/24 para 10. https://www.bundesgerichtshof.de/SharedDocs/Pressemitteilungen/DE/2024/2024093.html#:~:text=Der%20Bundesgerichtshof%20%2D%20Presse%20%3A%20Pressemitteilungen%20aus,auf%207%2C5%20g%20fest.

a significant amount. Hence, in legal practice, if a person is stopped by the police with 80 grams of cannabis with an active ingredient content of 10% THC (i.e., a total of 8 grams THC), the judges must take this significant quantity into account as an aggravating factor during sentencing. If the THC content is lower, sentencing must be adjusted accordingly.

With the new law and the decriminalization of large quantities of the drug, this threshold posed a problem. The German legislature saw this problem, and in an explanatory memorandum to the Cannabis Act, it had written that the threshold of 7.5 grams of THC would have to be significantly higher under the new law. The reason for this is obvious: According to the new law, a person is allowed to keep 50 grams of cannabis at home. Only when possessing more than 60 grams is a crime committed (§ 34 I). Hence, the 7.5 grams THC are quickly reached, assuming a purity of 10% to 15% THC. As a result, the law would immediately escalate from a completely legal amount to an aggravated case. This becomes even more problematic given the fact it is very difficult, if not impossible, for home growers to keep track of the exact quantities and the THC content of their plants. Given that the entire purpose of the cannabis law was to decriminalize and encourage growing the soft drug at home instead of turning to the illegal black market, it seems clear that a certain leeway and discretion had to be built into the law.

However, the German Bundesgerichtshof saw no reason to deviate from the decades old threshold of 7.5 grams THC. The court argued that this was based on objective criteria, and from a scientific perspective, the dangerousness of cannabis had not changed just because the legislature decided to partly decriminalize it. In fact, the legislature could have simply defined by law where the new threshold value of significant quantities should be set. However, since it did not do this but merely included a rather vague remark in the explanatory memorandum explicitly leaving the definition to the courts, it should come as no surprise if the courts make use of their discretion and rely on their own case law. Critics accused the court of intentionally ignoring the legislators' will as well as breaking constitutional law. It remains to be seen what effect this case law will have in the future.

Cannabis and Money Laundering

The third significant problem area that arises with the new cannabis law is its relationship to money laundering regulations. This problem was first pointed out by the legal scholar El-Ghazi.[23] Cultivating cannabis at home is time-consuming, costly, and not a realistic option for many consumers. It has

23 El-Ghazi, M. (2024). Cannabis-Konsumenten droht Verfolgung wegen Geldwäsche. *Legal Tribune Online*. https://www.lto.de/recht/hintergruende/h/cannabis-geldwaesche-entkriminalisierung-legalisierung-erwerb-schwarzmarkt-kcang/.

already been mentioned that the legislature has therefore authorized the possession of 25 grams (or 50 grams at home), even if the drug comes from illegal sources, i.e., was bought from black-market dealers. The problem, however, is that the legislature has overlooked the fact that while the purchase of cannabis from the black market may be legal under the Cannabis Act, this purchase still qualifies as money laundering. Since the legal reform in 2021, money laundering has become a so-called *all-weather crime* in Germany, according to which a person is criminally liable if s/he obtains an object that originates from any criminal offense. Even taking a piece of chocolate from a bar that someone else has previously stolen qualifies as money laundering.

Applied to the cannabis example: The black-market customer buys weed that originates from illicit commercial cultivation and, hence, still constitutes a criminal offense under the new cannabis law. Consumers should keep their hands off this illegally contaminated black-market cannabis to avoid committing money laundering. The future will show how law enforcement authorities will deal with this and whether cannabis users will soon find themselves increasingly exposed to prosecution for money laundering. If so, the aim of the law to reduce the workload of the police and judiciary would certainly be missed.

The Amount of 25 Grams of Cannabis

An issue that sparked controversial debates in the wake of the new German cannabis bill was the plan to decriminalize the possession of 25 grams of cannabis for consumers. The amount easily translates to approximately 75 joints or an amount a fairly regular consumer may use up in six months. Particularly, the critique was voiced from the side of law enforcement that feared a crucial problem: How to distinguish consumers in possession of 25 grams of weed from small-time street dealers? The amount is enough to provide street dealers with a good profit, and by re-stashing regularly, the illicit business may flourish with little to no risk at all of being caught by the police. This leaves the question of why the German legislature opted to let people carry around a six-month supply of weed when it creates the risk of blurring the distinction between consumers and dealers. Wouldn't it have sufficed to limit that amount to, for example, 10 grams or even lower, more than enough for personal use for an evening in the park or at a party? Moreover, it begs the question of whether the German legislature may have overstretched the boundaries of what still qualifies as a quantity for personal use privileged under EU law.

Already in Chapter 4, it was established that the EU Framework Decision 2004/757/Jha introduced in Article 2(2) the criterion of possession of drugs for personal consumption, which can be exempt from punishment. Instead of specifying what amount of a certain drug qualifies for personal consumption and which does not, the Framework Decision states that this is defined by national law. Indeed, the member states made use of that possibility with, for example, Lithuania allowing for 0.25 grams, Malta allowing for the possession of 7 grams of cannabis, and the Dutch limiting the daily amount that can be purchased in a coffee shop to 5 grams per person. The German Federal Court already in 1995 established the amount of 6 grams as a small amount that most likely is for personal consumption only and hence could be exempt from prosecution. While there is little consistency between the EU member states, it appears that the amount of 25 grams is unprecedented, and no other country even comes close to this amount.[24] This is even the case for Portugal, as was already mentioned, where in practice, an amount of 25 grams may be allowed but legally spread over ten days, resulting in 2.5 grams per day. Curiously enough a look at Wikipedia and the English version of the article 'Cannabis in Portugal' explains that the 'Possession of cannabis in Portugal is decriminalised in amounts for personal use, considered to be up to 25 g of plant material'.[25]

While technically correct, from a legal point of view, this statement is at least imprecise as the 25 grams refers to a ten-day amount. Did the drafters of the German cannabis law consult Wikipedia in order to assess what the highest possible amount for personal consumption may be? Since the CJEU has left this open and Portugal has gotten away with this for almost two decades, it seems only logical to assume that the 25 grams is in compliance with EU law. However, unlike the Portuguese legislature, the German cannabis law did not include the ten-day limit for the possession of 25 grams. As to why this is, one can only speculate since the allowed possession of 50 grams at home is actually a monthly limit. Of course, the question of how to control and legally enforce this monthly limit in practice remains completely in the dark, just as has been the case with the ten-day limit in Portugal.

Broken Promises?

This book begins with the heated dialogue in October 2022 on German public TV between German Health Minister Karl Lauterbach and talk show host Markus Lanz, who cannot be convinced that legalizing cannabis is a good idea. Lauterbach promised that if the European Commission did not approve his plans, he would not pursue a full legalization of cannabis. As is often the case in politics and especially in drug policy, in a paradoxical reflex, Lauterbach has both kept and broken his promise at the same time. He kept his promise because the law he originally had in mind was significantly downgraded after consultations with the European Commission. Hence, he was not

24 EMCDDA. (2023). *Cannabis laws in Europe: Questions and answers for policymaking* (p. 22), June. https://www.emcdda.europa.eu/publications/faq/cannabis-laws-europe-questions-and-answers-for-policymaking_en.

25 See at https://en.wikipedia.org/wiki/Cannabis_in_Portugal.

the one making the law, i.e., a full legalization of cannabis in Germany. But in the eyes of many opponents of cannabis legalization, Lauterbach broke his promise to cancel the legalization project entirely. Instead, the health minister seemed to have taken up the challenge of pushing the boundaries of what is still in compliance with EU law to its limits. The result is one of, if not the most far-reaching regulation of cannabis in Europe.

Still, legalization advocates were disappointed, arguing the health minister did not fulfill his promise. Their argument: The European Commission never disapproved of a full legalization, at least not officially. The compliance of national law with EU law is assessed through a notification procedure. If that procedure results in a conflict between the member state and the Commission, the ultimate decision will lie with the CJEU. The initial German plans never made it to the notification procedure but were suffocated through informal (and secretive) consultations.

This process left behind a legal vacuum. What if the European Commission had to assess the full legalization of cannabis as Germany had initially planned? How would they have responded to the concrete regulations? With which arguments would they have disapproved which regulations? Would there have been room to revise certain parts? And if not, would it have been worth it to address the CJEU? How would the Court have decided on the German regulative approach? We won't know, at least for the time being. What is even more disappointing from a regulative point of view is that if a German bill had ended up before the EU's highest court, it might have taken the chance to sketch out the reliable legal framework for how and to what extent cannabis can be regulated in the EU. This would result in more legal certainty for the member states and, above all, for EU citizens. In that sense, we have missed the chance of being provided with a blueprint for drug policy reform in Europe.

A Risky Business

'I consider this to be highly risky'. This was the title of the interview I gave to the well-known German news magazine *DER SPIEGEL* in May 2022. The statement caused some fierce reactions among legalization advocates – at least among those who had only read the title and not the entire interview. By 'highly risky', I did not mean the legalization of cannabis per se or health risks for consumers. What I considered risky, then as I do now, was the legal strategy of enacting a law that very likely breaks EU law in order to force the CJEU to take a landmark decision. The risk lies in the high probability of Germany losing the case before the court, which would trigger at least two consequences: Firstly, the negative court decision would not only have set clear limits for further legalization efforts. Final judgments are binding and form the case law for a considerable part of the future until the court overturns its own jurisprudence.

Secondly, in the time between the enactment of the law and a final decision by the court, a dynamic would have likely been set off, and the consequences would have been difficult to anticipate. Companies and cannabis start-ups would have made considerable investments in anticipation of a legalized cannabis market. Sales outlets would have established themselves, and as consumers had not to fear any persecution, a flourishing trade in legal, semi-legal, and illegal cannabis would have developed. At the same time, however, the establishment of control bodies to monitor the fast-growing market would have progressed slowly in view of the uncertainty as to whether legalization would hold up before the CJEU, and there would not have been much hurry to create new authorities and bodies. In case the CJEU had overturned the cannabis law, the German state would not only have run the risk of being held liable for damages for investments made in reliance on the validity of the new law. The judiciary and law enforcement authorities would also have had their hands full restoring law and order, a difficult task given that some dynamics cannot simply be rewound. The German taxpayer would have had to bear the costs of such an experiment.

In view of the socio-political dimension of the legalization plans and their potential societal impacts, it seemed important to me to at least name these risks. The decision of how to proceed was still left to the legislature. Nevertheless, this stance has earned me a lot of criticism, interestingly enough mainly from other legal scholars. One well-known authority in the field even accused me of being responsible for the full legalization of cannabis in Germany being called off. I consider this as perhaps one of the best and, at the same time, most ridiculous compliments I have ever received. The best is not because preventing legalization was close to my heart – quite the opposite – but because I think it's great when scientists apparently have a voice that is heard in the political arena. However, the statement is ridiculous in the sense that it is completely absurd that a scholar like me merely pointing out the legal risks should be solely responsible for the German government putting one of the most progressive and far-reaching drug policy projects of the last 50 years on ice.

At its core, this is a misunderstanding that many scientists today have fallen victim to, not only in law but in many other scientific fields as well. In scientific thinking, the Bayesian approach is something like a compass in giving guidance and direction. The approach is about reasoning in the face of uncertainty and expressing scientific validity in probabilities. It means while sciences should strive to be as objective as possible, scientific results can never be 100% accurate. These lines are written in the middle of June, and while the probability of tomorrow having sunshine might be high, it is not 100% sure. On the other hand, the probability of negative degrees tomorrow and a snowstorm raging over the country is extremely low – but the chance is not zero. A scientist, more precisely a meteorologist, telling you he is absolutely certain there will not be rain tomorrow is either lying or does not understood

Bayesian thinking. Or his predictions are guided by his own idiosyncrasies as he might have long planned a picnic in the park with the family, and he really wishes for sunshine. Indeed, personal idiosyncrasies and wishful thinking are the enemy of scientific objectivity, but since all scientists are human, there is no scientific reasoning without some subjectivity. Hence, scientific reasoning is communicated through probabilities rather than certainties. This, of course, applies to legal assessments as well and does not contradict the fact that different experts can come to different risk assessments.

What does this mean for cannabis and the risks related to forcing an CJEU ruling on full legalization? ‘On the high seas and before the court, one’s fate is in God’s hand’. This famous saying, often quoted by lawyers to their clients, sums up the difficulty of anticipating a court decision. However, facing this uncertainty makes scientific reasoning even more important, while it is paramount to avoid substituting the uncertainty for personal beliefs about right or wrong or what allegedly is good or bad for society. The latter runs the risk of blurring the lines between scientific reasoning and political activism. I cannot stress this enough: While we all might have our convictions about the necessity of drug policy reform, these are rather irrelevant when it comes to assessing the legal risks of implementing the legalization of cannabis.

Legalization Through the Backdoor?

Let us, for the last time, revisit the exchange between the German health minister and the journalist Markus Lanz at the beginning of this book. The talk show host claims that the German Health Minister Karl Lauterbach was arguing against his own inner convictions. But how did Lanz know what is going on in Lauterbach’s head? How would he anticipate his real motivations? Perhaps he didn’t, and he is just trying to lure his interviewee out of his reserve. But what if Lanz was right? What if Lauterbach never really believed in the benefits of legalizing recreational cannabis? While this first may sound unlikely, on closer examination, there could be some truth to this.

While the new German cannabis law undoubtedly introduced some far-reaching changes for the consumers of recreational cannabis, it also has some significant implications for medical cannabis. These are so significant that some commentators would even call it a legalization through the backdoor.[26] While, according to the new law, medical cannabis remains subject to prescription, the thresholds for doctors to prescribe it have become much lower and are comparable to prescribing ibuprofen painkillers. While until then, cannabis was prescribed only as a last resort when other medicines did not help, this ultima ratio approach was scrapped. While this makes access to cannabis much easier for patients, it seems that many doctors are rather

26 Sobota, 2024, 1220; Oğlakcıoğlu & Welke, 2024, 204.

reluctant to prescribe cannabis flowers for pain therapy. There are a number of reasons for this, with the most important one being that the scientific evidence for the effectiveness of cannabis as a painkiller remains, to date, rather thin.

The new cannabis law opens a backdoor for cannabis consumers by making it fairly easy to get their hands on medical cannabis. With telemedicine doctors who specialize in cannabis prescriptions supported by shady pseudo-medical companies providing apps to link consumers with these doctors, everyone can become a cannabis patient. These services are not for free, and some may feel reminded of the dubious and highly dangerous 'pill mills' in the US, with doctors basically selling prescriptions for opiates with no or very little indication, triggering the opioid crisis and costing the lives of hundreds of thousands of Americans. While these medical 'cannabis mills' are far from having the same deadly impact, it may only be a matter of time before authorities will put an end to these dubious practices.

The young German medical cannabis industry is rejoicing. In the wake of a law aimed at recreational use and with all the controversy revolving around the scope of decriminalization, the small revolution in the medical cannabis market has floated along without causing much of a stir. Surely, some would consider this legalization through the backdoor as a pragmatic approach to ensure the supply of cannabis to consumers. The quality standards of the products are high, and the profits don't end with black-market dealers. Hence, it is a win-win for everyone involved, but above all, for the minister of health, who will surely be thanked by producers, pharmacies, and consumers. From this perspective, it is even forgivable that the announced and highly anticipated full legalization ultimately was watered down to partial decriminalization.

From a regulatory and drug policy reform perspective, this approach seems half-baked. There is a certain irony in the fact that Germany created a backdoor problem of its own. One that certainly does not reach the dimensions of the situation in the Netherlands, but at least in the long term, might potentially jeopardize the acceptance of the new cannabis policy. The reputational damage the drug may suffer through the systematic abuse of medical cannabis for recreational use gives powerful ammunition to any subsequent government striving to reverse the new cannabis regulations.

Index

For Product Safety Concerns and Information please contact our EU representative GPSR@taylorandfrancis.com
Taylor & Francis Verlag GmbH, Kaufingerstraße 24, 80331 München, Germany

www.ingramcontent.com/pod-product-compliance
Ingram Content Group UK Ltd.
Pitfield, Milton Keynes, MK11 3LW, UK
UKHW020942210926
475569UK00020B/11

* 9 7 8 1 0 3 2 8 2 2 0 3 7 *